Own This!

Own This!

How Platform Cooperatives Help Workers Build a Democratic Internet

R. Trebor Scholz

VERSO

London • New York

First published by Verso 2023
© R. Trebor Scholz 2023

1 3 5 7 9 10 8 6 4 2

Verso
UK: 6 Meard Street, London W1F 0EG
US: 388 Atlantic Avenue, Brooklyn, NY 11217
versobooks.com

Verso is the imprint of New Left Books

ISBN-13: 978-1-83976-455-4
ISBN-13: 978-1-83976-458-5 (UK EBK)
ISBN-13: 978-1-83976-457-8 (US EBK)

British Library Cataloguing in Publication Data
A catalogue record for this book is available from the British Library

Library of Congress Cataloging-in-Publication Data

Names: Scholz, R. Trebor, author.
Title: Own this! : how platform cooperatives help workers build a
    democratic Internet / R. Trebor Scholz.
Description: London ; New York : Verso, 2023. | Includes bibliographical
    references and index.
Identifiers: LCCN 2023020763 (print) | LCCN 2023020764 (ebook) | ISBN
    9781839764561 (hardback) | ISBN 9781839764585 (ebook)
Subjects: LCSH: Multi-sided platform businesses. | Cooperative societies. |
    Employee ownership. | Democracy.
Classification: LCC HD9999.M782 S36 2023 (print) | LCC HD9999.M782
    (ebook) | DDC 338.7—dc23/eng/20230602
LC record available at https://lccn.loc.gov/2023020763
LC ebook record available at https://lccn.loc.gov/2023020764

Typeset in Fournier by Biblichor Ltd, Scotland
Printed and bound by CPI Group (UK) Ltd, Croydon CR0 4YY

Contents

1

Alternative Paths

Derick Ongansie, a former Uber driver turned labor activist, greeted me at Cape Town International Airport a few years ago. In his late fifties, Ongansie had a strong voice, a thick beard, and a denim shirt, giving him a unique no-nonsense appearance. He told me about the predicament of Uber drivers in South Africa, the majority of whom are foreign African migrants, who regard the company as a "platform of fear." Since being "deactivated" (fired) is permanent in South Africa, it is a continuous source of concern. Ongansie offered me some background. The Uber Drivers Guild was established in April 2016 by a group of South African Uber drivers, which he led. At the time, 2,000 of the 10,000 registered drivers in South Africa had joined. The Guild sued the ride-hailing firm, claiming employee status for the taxi drivers, with the assistance of a team of lawyers. The defecting cabbies also enlisted the help of a public union, and the two groups worked together to win the case. The drivers won their suit in the first instance, but then lost on appeal. Unfortunately, since Uber has such deep coffers, it was able to hire additional attorneys to prolong the legal battle, which the union could no longer afford. Around that time, Ongansie contacted me, asking for my assistance in forming a cooperative, tentatively named CabNet

Technology. Through his work with the Uber Drivers Guild in Cape Town, Ongansie recognized that the kind of funding and effort expended on strikes and lawsuits could have potentially been used by the drivers to establish their own ventures. They could change the system through worker self-management and ownership.

Wages for drivers like Ongansie had always been meager, but recently, with COVID-19, business had suddenly dropped, putting their livelihoods in jeopardy.[1] With the pandemic, more activities such as remote work, learning, and basic human interaction were moving to digital platforms. And it was all correlated with the numbers in the bank accounts of Silicon Valley executives, particularly those in charge of platforms that do not rely on human contact.

Worldwide, at least 40 million individuals have, at least once, worked and earned money through apps. Workers who find "gigs" in this manner are predominantly migrants and other marginalized individuals. Beyond the couriers and taxi drivers, there are people cleaning apartments, caring for elders, or laboring along the global tech supply chains. Already before the pandemic, digital platform companies heavily relied on such low-paid labor. They depend on minorities, migrants, and other individuals who face disadvantages in their societies because of caste, poverty, disability, gender, or race. Often, these workers remain out of sight.

And it is not only that these workers are disproportionately more at risk (they are). They also experience an even more extreme lack of workplace democracy than people in the analog workplace, where they at least have the opportunity to directly interact with their bosses. The cultural critic Raymond Williams argued that liberal democracy suffered from a peculiar blind spot that valued "educated and participatory democracy" at the national constitutional level while rarely translating that into institutional norms and templates.[2] As Williams observed, the twentieth century saw a wave of countries embracing democracy as their preferred political model. And yet the system in which most people spend the majority of their time—the world of work—is run according to a different set of rules.

Here, they have to spend their lives in servitude to a boss, in a form of subordination that dictates to them when they may go to the bathroom, what clothes they must wear, and how they should behave when they encounter an unpleasant customer. It is called having a job. This kind of subordination was exacerbated by Taylorism, a scientific management approach to increase efficiency and productivity, involving the development of a technique of surveillance in which the manager would control every movement a worker makes. Today's methods of workplace surveillance are far more invasive than those of the early twentieth century—let's say in Amazon's warehouses, where a worker's location is known at all times.

What is so surprising about this kind of management is that it is understood as common sense. Young people are told that they have to ready themselves for the job market, and gaining employment becomes one of the highest goals in life. What if, instead, people could express themselves, driven by self-guided energy and inventiveness? It is worth pondering how to change a system based on the domination of others, which is an attack on human dignity.[3]

And what is valid for the workplaces that Williams refers to is even more relevant when examining centralized digital labor platforms with global reach.

What is the main cause of workplace assaults on dignity and basic rights? Focusing too much on the fortunes of industry leaders like Mukesh Ambani and Jeff Bezos diverts attention away from the fact that this issue in the platform economy is inherent in the for-profit corporation as an organizational paradigm. The predicament of drivers like Derick Ongansie is what you get when you push the logic at the heart of the corporate model to the extreme.

The pandemic is a cautionary tale about the consequences of unbridled privatization of ownership in sectors that millions of people depend on. The economic model of coordinating vital services used by venture capital–backed digital platforms exemplifies the ownership problem. A board of directors, senior management, and shareholders run and govern major-league tech companies. One report states:

> Boards are legally prohibited from prioritizing community or societal interests above the financial interests of shareholders . . . Instead, companies are incentivized—and often obligated—to make whatever decisions will maximize shareholder profits without sharing those returns with workers or affected communities.[4]

This ownership model is part of the reason for the democracy blind spot that Raymond Williams laid bare.

The chief executives of such businesses are not the ones attempting to earn a livelihood via companies such as Deliveroo, Upwork, and Uber. Given the mistreatment of workers that we have just described, we may start to consider redesigning ownership for the digital economy. Collective ownership, self-governance, and worker self-control have a long history, dating back to the kibbutzim of the region of Palestine in the early 1900s, as well as to the short-lived period between 1936 and 1939 primarily in Catalonia, Aragon, and Andalusia during the Spanish Civil War, and to the Zapatistas starting in the early 1980s in the southern Mexican state of Chiapas.[5]

Today, countries all around the globe are working to establish their own Silicon Valleys, often with little regard for worker autonomy. They want to re-create a culture of single-entrepreneur heroism that does not adequately serve the public good. In the United States, amid this culture, Black entrepreneurs receive a startling 1 percent of total venture capital investment, while all-female founder teams secure just a single-digit percentage of VC funding.

To this depiction of venture capital (VC) culture, I would add that the founders are pouring all of their passion and energy into companies over which they will lose control if they do not produce profits fast enough. If a start-up is not profitable after a few short years, a venture investor probably will take control of it, which can be devastating for the entrepreneurs. VC-fueled entrepreneurship frequently pursues a speedy exit rather than establishing a company that will sustain its stakeholders in the long run, contradicting the founders' initial vision or purpose.

It is all about selling the company, the workers, and the platform users to the highest bidder as soon as the first chance arises. Another aspect of this is that the buyer may either repurpose the acquired company's intellectual property for their own products (thus consolidating their market position), or simply use the acquisition to shut down the business (i.e., nipping competition in the bud).

The pandemic has served as a litmus test. It has highlighted even more clearly the need to shift the ownership of the modern corporation. Experiments with collective ownership are one way forward. What if digital platforms were cooperatively owned? What if communities, including users and workers, had ownership and governance over the algorithms and servers of digital platforms, as well as upstream services? And, what if the overall internet infrastructure were ultimately owned by the public or public-cooperative hybrids? One recurring objection is that if you want to "own" a company, why not just buy shares in it? Aside from the issue of affordability, shared ownership is a considerably more limited form of ownership than cooperative ownership, because the latter is not restricted to corporate governance decisions. Cooperative ownership can allow members to have a say in day-to-day operational decisions, such as the design of a product, in addition to big business decisions such as electing a director or increasing the price for services.

And this is not only because of the concentration of power and wealth in the hands of the most prominent tech companies. The recent renaissance of cooperatives can be attributed, at least in part, to the challenges posed by authoritarian regimes and dysfunctional governments in many countries, with cooperative models offering a partial but readily available shield for workers. In Brazil, the police under President Jair Bolsonaro threatened and killed Black people; in Turkey, President Recep Tayyip Erdoğan put thousands of his critics behind bars; concerns about democratic norms and the rule of law have been raised in Israel; in Poland and Hungary, right-wing parties have been accused of undermining democratic institutions; and in the United States, Donald Trump catastrophically mismanaged the government's response to the pandemic, and today the public's trust in the government in the country remains low, with only two out of ten Americans believing that the government in Washington will do the right thing "almost always" or "most of the time" (19 percent).[6] How can people trust their governments if the solutions proposed by politicians in these countries are too incremental or show indifference toward the needs of the population and do not make a significant impact in their daily lives? Therefore, but without giving up on the project of electoral politics (!), people are turning to practices of mutual aid, and to cooperatives in particular.

Co-ops are one way to diversify the digital economy and to respond to the extreme lack of workplace democracy and the varying degrees of exploitation on digital platforms. To traverse the shifting world of technology and innovation, it is also important to craft new narratives that encourage experimentation and rethink ownership and entrepreneurial culture. The reality is that the next big thing may not be just one model, but rather a combination of different approaches, which one scholar has referred to as a bricolage of organizational models.[7] Unions are an important part of this bricolage, having made some inroads in gig economy struggles already. It is worth mentioning the history of union co-ops, too, in this context, which dates back to the Reconstruction era in the United States from 1865 to 1867, following the American Civil War. In the 1870s and '80s, the Knights of Labor launched countless cooperatives to create strike funds and at one point had a membership of 700,000 union members. In addition to unions, the current landscape of organizations experimenting with ownership also includes steward-owned enterprises and employee stock ownership plans. The question then becomes how to adapt these organizational forms, such as cooperatives and union co-ops, to the digital economy. How can we create interlocking organizational forms, or a bricolage, to fit the unique challenges and opportunities of the digital age?[8]

How likely is it that cooperative principles will live up to the challenges posed by the digital economy? In times of crisis, transformations that once appeared inconceivable might suddenly become common sense, such as the emergence of cooperatives and unions in response to the Industrial Revolution and their global spread over the past 200 years, or the New Deal carried out by Franklin D. Roosevelt. Considering these examples, it is reasonable to suggest that the Overton window may change, rendering cooperative principles a viable approach to the challenges posed by the digital economy.

Platform Co-ops

In this time of digital transition, I propose a people-centric approach that prioritizes participatory processes and centers the voices and needs of those who depend on the internet the most, envisioning a future where they have greater control over its apps, platforms, and protocols. Picture a federation-led ride-hailing platform that utilizes not only its technological know-how but also its convening power to support worker cooperatives of taxi drivers on a global scale. Picture a scenario in which inner-city communities collaborate to implement high-speed internet infrastructure cooperatively, potentially bridging the digital divide for households like the 88,820 in Manhattan who currently lack such connectivity.[9] Imagine a world in which social media platforms are owned and managed by their users. Instead of a few giant conglomerates holding immense power over our personal data and online interaction, the users themselves would be capable of deciding on the governance and new features of the platform. Or, what about launching cooperatives offering food-delivery services jointly owned by the couriers, restaurant owners, and foodies? Now consider that more than 543 self-managed and cooperatively owned businesses in forty-nine countries prove that such a cooperative ecosystem is not a figment of the utopian imagination, but a fact already today.[10]

A "platform cooperative" refers to a project or business that *primarily* uses a website, mobile app, or protocol to sell goods (e.g., data) or services, and relies on democratic decision-making and shared community ownership of the platform by workers and users. Not all platform cooperatives are incorporated as formal cooperatives. And, of course, this definition of platform cooperatives is a dynamic and evolving one, representing a process of becoming rather than a fixed or singular model. As we are talking about definitions: In the context of this book, a digital platform is an online infrastructure that facilitates interactions and exchanges among individuals and groups, with the capacity to coordinate activities and extract data to generate revenue, while simultaneously promoting scalability. It encompasses a broad range of online applications, protocols, and web-based systems used for connecting or organizing services and has emerged as the predominant mode of economic organization.

And what about cooperatives? People may know cooperatives because they buy their cheese, milk, or juice from farming cooperatives. They may live in a housing co-op or shop in consumer cooperatives for their camping equipment or hardware. And they want to see a continuation of this model that is so dear to their hearts.

The International Cooperative Alliance, the global steward of the cooperative movement, defines cooperatives as "autonomous associations of persons united voluntarily to meet their common economic, social, and cultural needs and aspirations through a jointly owned and democratically controlled enterprise."[11] They are created by people who have a need that is not addressed. They come together to set up a company that will meet that need. I will say more about cooperatives, but let me first stay with platform co-ops and outline the sectors in which they are most prominent. I will then introduce Drivers Cooperative, a platform co-op in New York City.

The ecosystem of platform co-ops is composed of an array of businesses, including small and medium-sized projects, as well as some with a per-annum turnover exceeding $200 million and close to 300 employees, and many just starting with a business plan on paper, three founders, and a cat. They may be incorporated as cooperatives, or they may function like co-ops while using the limited liability company (LLC) as a form of incorporation, especially in countries where incorporation as a cooperative is not possible. While some platform co-ops are cooperatives with a digital twist, others represent entirely new models of cooperative ownership that look vastly different from traditional cooperatives. As we will see, they go far beyond groups of 1960s college students sharing a house and doling out cooking and cleaning responsibilities.

Just as the co-op model does not make sense in all contexts, platform co-ops are likely to benefit some sectors more than others. Platform co-ops come in many forms and sizes, making them too complex to be captured in a straightforward manner, although some scholars have attempted to create frameworks. Currently, platform co-ops are found in the transportation sector, as we have learned from Derick Ongansie. Some platform co-ops focus on local gig work, cultural services, data and infrastructure, or asset sharing, and they appear in sectors ranging from agriculture and finance to home services, software development, transportation, insurance, care, and more. Let's just take the care sector, which is especially prone to industry-wide organizational transformations based on cooperative principles. The proportion of Americans aged sixty-five and older, the group that requires the most care, will increase from 16 percent to 23 percent between 2018 and 2060.[12] Women are overrepresented, undervalued, and underpaid as workers in the care sector, which is one of the fastest-growing in the US. Home caregivers work unpredictable hours and earn about $16,000 per year.[13] While the low likelihood of automation in eldercare should make these jobs more attractive to people, the reality is that the low pay of these positions often discourages potential workers, making it crucial to bring more appreciation and funding to this sector. A cooperative approach to ownership and governance of care platforms could bring dignity and fair pay to this profession, while also making it easier to pair workers with nearby clients and organize members, clients, and workers across territories.

The global ecosystem of platform co-ops involves more than just local and transnational gig work. Think of the global ecosystem of platform co-ops as a well-coordinated system, where labor platforms, social media, and web infrastructure operate in perfect sync. Labor platforms function as generators, while social media and other internet platforms act as the circuits, all guided by cooperative principles, working toward a more fair and democratic internet.

Platform cooperatives combines the proven cooperative model, which has been embraced by one billion people worldwide, with the thriving digital platform model, which continues to thrive despite the tech lash. This model also includes distributed technologies, resulting in the potential for wider adoption and greater impact in spreading the benefits of cooperatives to more people than the traditional brick-and-mortar model of cooperatives.

Many platform co-ops, such as Up & Go and Equal Care Co-op in the United Kingdom, pay their workers twice as much as similar VC-styled platforms, highlighting the benefits of this approach, particularly for worker co-ops and multi-stakeholder co-ops. These cooperatives have also experienced an increase in productivity among their workers, who now have a stake in their companies. They want to participate. And not just that: They are their own bosses, even if there is a management layer. Managers in worker cooperatives are not only elected by the workers themselves but are also accountable to the members and can be fired by them; their responsibility lies in executing the rules that the members have voted on. With this approach, platform cooperatives aim to create a more inclusive and democratic economy in which decision-making power is shared. They prioritize community benefit over profit extraction, resulting in a more sustainable and equitable model of business that generates value for the community and provides long-term value for both founders and workers, as opposed to Uber drivers in Cape Town who generate profits for shareholders thousands of miles away. Faiza Haupt, originally known as the first female Uber driver in South Africa, has become a pioneer in Cape Town's ride-hailing platform cooperative, along with Ongansie. They have joined forces to create a cooperative business model that ensures that revenue stays in the local community. Also, platform cooperatives, unlike certain tech colossi, prioritize paying taxes locally instead of diverting funds through tax havens or low-tax jurisdictions.

Through my conversations with workers like Ongansie and Haupt, I have discovered that being a part of a platform cooperative not only provides them with a concrete sense of dignity but also makes their lives more predictable and manageable. Members know what their income will be next week. Platform cooperatives are not guided by opaque algorithms, or the infamous "algorithmic boss," and a large number of them have been co-designed by the platforms' users to ensure that their design considers the requirements of those who rely on them the most.

And because they own the platform, they can be open about if and how they collect and manage data, which may provide them with a competitive edge. Because they own the platform and therefore—to an extent—control the flow of data, they can provide greater privacy than comparable businesses.

Cooperatives have been founded by both anti-capitalists and people looking for a way to make ends meet since their inception, covering the entire political spectrum and emphasizing the importance of lived experience over political views, providing a rare opportunity for people from diverse backgrounds to find common ground amid growing political polarization.

Despite their merits, platform co-ops face significant barriers, particularly in terms of start-up financing, which is already a major hurdle for traditional tech start-up entrepreneurs and becomes even more onerous for cooperative enterprises, reminiscent of the struggles faced by legacy cooperatives. This may come as a surprise, given cooperatives' almost 200-year track record. Still, investors' hesitancy to invest in nontraditional businesses, potentially also linked to their class positionality, has resulted in a preference for businesses that align with prevailing norms and avoid challenging established ownership structures. Despite the false perception held by some investors and individuals that cooperatives are antiquated and uncreative, legacy co-ops have a strong presence in countries such as Italy, Finland, and Kenya, where they dominate entire regions and sectors. Despite prejudice against the idea that working-class immigrants are capable of running a tech platform, platform co-ops have a strong show of force not only in the US and Europe but also, more and more, in the so-called Global South. But even in countries celebrated for their cooperative heritage, the prevalence of male managers of a certain age, alongside a graying membership, highlights the need to forge pathways for younger generations, immigrants, and individuals of gender-expansive identities and diverse sexual orientations to assume co-op leadership roles, all while urgently and meaning-fully embracing technology. And some idealistic founders face bottlenecks in running a thriving enterprise as they prioritize governance and democratic decision-making over developing a compelling value proposition.

Later in this book, I'll be discussing how to scale cooperative tech models in light of the significant network effects and finan-cial advantages of large tech companies, and also the fact that younger generations often view platform co-ops as a viable substi-tute for these tech giants, rendering this scaling of solidarity and co-op values an especially intriguing topic. People in the plat-form co-op movement, both founders and members, aspire to a set of values based on the long history of cooperatives in all of these various industries. On December 21, 1844, the Rochdale Soci-ety of Equitable Pioneers was founded in the North of England. Because there were no laws allowing for formal incorporation as a cooperative at the time, this early consumer cooperative was not officially recognized as such, but it was one of the first to pay a patronage dividend, forming the basis of the modern cooperative movement. Other co-ops had preceded it, but the Rochdale Pioneers formulated principles that later served as guidelines for cooperatives worldwide.

The International Cooperative Alliance (ICA), founded half a century later, formulated its set of principles in 1937 based on the principles of the Rochdale Pioneers, revising them over time. Today, these principles read as follows:

- Voluntary and open membership
- Democratic member control
- Member economic participation
- Autonomy and independence
- Education, training, and information
- Cooperation among cooperatives
- Concern for the community.

In this book, I will explore how cooperative principles, both in traditional settings and online platforms, have supported all those who have confronted unemployment, advocating for workplace democracy, and working toward a fairer and more democratic internet, benefiting not only workers but all who inhabit the online landscape.

Driving Toward Fair Labor

One way of giving you a flavor of this movement is to look to New York City, where Erik Forman, a labor organizer and doctoral student; Ken Lewis, a Grenadian transportation professional; and Alissa Orlando, a former operations manager for Uber in East Africa came together in May 2020 to found the Drivers Cooperative, a worker-owned platform co-op for ride-hailing.

Given the economic strain brought on by the pandemic, the Drivers Cooperative has made it a priority to revolutionize the ride-sharing sector by focusing on the need for higher pay for drivers. The platform co-op has enlisted more than 9,000 drivers, 91 percent of whom are immigrants, and has raised $2.4 million through a combination of loans and crowdfunding. The cooperative's maiden passengers were early voters, their rides arranged by the campaign of Alexandria Ocasio-Cortez, a progressive member of the United States House of Representatives, and since then, the Drivers Cooperative has provided over 200,000 rides to passengers. As a solidarity measure, the co-op pays drivers a base rate of $30 per hour, regardless of whether they have passengers or not.

Passengers who use the Drivers Cooperative pay a fare that is routinely lower than that of competitors, and there is no surge pricing. At Drivers Cooperative, members can participate in democratic decision-making, including the power to vote on significant matters. Beyond this, the Drivers Cooperative tackles issues such as exploitative loan rates for cars and arbitrary firings (what Uber deceivingly calls "deactivation"). The platform co-op also offers a free Driver Academy for ride-hailing, where taxi workers can share knowledge about cooperatives and tools. As part of its pledge of transparency and sustainability, the Drivers Cooperative intends to offer traffic and congestion data to cities that are routinely kept in the dark about the environmental impact of traditional ride-sharing companies.

The Drivers Cooperative is also advocating for a bill that mirrors New York City mayor Eric Adams's proposal for the Taxi and Limousine Commission, which aims to provide city subsidies to enable drivers to purchase electric vehicles. At the same time, Uber is cruising along, maxing out its market share thanks to a lack of profits, accountability, and transparency. Uber is staring down the barrel of its own failure to replace drivers with autonomous cars. Drivers for the ride-sharing giant have reported wage theft to the tune of hundreds of millions of dollars.[14]

Drivers Cooperative recognizes that it may not outperform Uber in the short term but acknowledges the importance of tertiary and quaternary competitors in the ride-hailing industry and has a long-term aspiration to build a global federation of platform co-ops in the ride-hailing sector. Already now, in one of the world's most competitive cities, Drivers Cooperative, driven by the determination of working-class immigrants, defies skeptical observers such as business professors, conservative policymakers, and foundation officers by proving that drivers can, in fact, own and operate a nonpredatory transportation company.

Origins

Drivers Cooperative is just one example of this new ecosystem that has emerged over the past years. With the emergence of companies like Drivers Cooperative, there has been a growing interest in "platform labor" and its impact on society. I began my intellectual exploration in this area in 2008, inspired by Italian Workerism. I proposed that people's activities on platforms such as MySpace be deemed "data labor." During my tenure at the New School in New York City, I organized numerous conferences and delivered countless presentations on the theme of digital labor and its broader impact. In 2013, I spoke in front of a large crowd at a media festival in Berlin, shedding light on the fact that novice workers on the crowd labor platform Amazon Mechanical Turk were earning an unconscionable $2 to $3 per hour. The presentation of the sobering realities of digital labor left both the audience and myself distressed, highlighting the need to move beyond the mere analysis of digital labor. This defining moment in Berlin revealed to me that there is an acute lack of responsive conceptual and practical frameworks for near-future alternatives that, if realized, could pave the way for a more equitable economy. VC-funded platform-based business models have been sharply denounced by many scholars, but solely analyzing the problem does not improve the circumstances of taxi drivers, care workers, or bicycle couriers.

A few months after my talk in Berlin, we found ourselves seated in a circle in the Woolman Auditorium, located on the top floor of the New School's Twelfth Street building in Greenwich Village. It was 2014, during the twelfth hour of the "Digital Labor: Sweatshops,

Picket Lines, Barricades" symposium that I had organized. And it was during this meeting that an experienced Amazon Mechanical Turk worker suggested, "Why don't we just create our own platform?" For me, this was a moment of sudden clarity in which my experience with cooperatives, research on digital labor, and upbringing in East Berlin all came together, merging my intellectual inquiry and lived experience.

As an experienced cooperative member, I have lived in a housing cooperative. As a member of the Old First Nursery School parent cooperative in Brooklyn, I sold Christmas trees during long weekends in December to support the co-op's financial needs. I am also a long-standing member of the Park Slope Food Cooperative, one of the oldest and largest food cooperatives in the United States. The Park Slope Food Cooperative positions itself as a buying agent for its members rather than a selling agent for any industry.[15] However, the *New Yorker* once described it, in tongue-in-cheek fashion, as "a user-friendly way of experiencing the pitfalls of communism" due to its strict regulations and mandatory work shifts for all members, highlighting the outside biases that co-ops often face, including the misconception that they are always associated with with left-leaning or anti-business ideologies.[16]

With memories of my cooperative experiences fresh in my mind, a spark ignited as I sat in the Woolman Auditorium in 2014: "Let's bring the cooperative model together with the platform economy." I stayed up all night and penned the essay "Platform Cooperativism vs. the Sharing Economy," which gave rise to the concept.[17] In a subsequent paper titled "Platform Cooperativism: Challenging the Corporate Sharing Economy," published by the Rosa Luxemburg Foundation (and ultimately translated into many languages), I further elaborated on the concept and proposed a set of principles for platform cooperatives, calling on their advocates to

- Co-design
- Offer decent pay
- Guarantee transparency in the collection of personal data
- Offer cross-platform portability of data
- Offer portable worker profiles.

A year later, in 2015, I organized a conference at the New School in collaboration with American academic and organizer Nathan Schneider. This event, which took place as part of a conference series I had been convening for the six years since its launch in 2009, marked a significant milestone in the movement's journey. Janelle Orsi, a lawyer, cartoonist, and proponent of communal ownership, was invited to give the keynote address. She advocated for a "new sharing economy" based on cooperative ownership. It was a timely and intense event, with a thousand people in the crowd and an outpouring of deep-felt support from the tens of thousands watching online, yearning to resist the exploitative nature of what was dubbed as a "sharing economy." Many participants left the event to establish platform cooperatives in their home countries. A year later, shortly after the publication of my book *Uberworked and Underpaid*, which discussed the exploitative nature of the gig economy and introduced platform cooperatives, Schneider and I co-edited the collection *Ours to Hack and to Own: The Rise of Platform Cooperativism, a New Vision for the Future of Work and a Fairer Internet*. And soon after, I took a leap and founded the Platform Cooperativism Consortium (PCC)—an organization dedicated to fostering the growth of platform co-ops and related projects. With a strong commitment to collective knowledge-building and community-engaged research, the PCC strives to build global community, encourage coordination, develop resources, and conduct policy analysis.

Of course, there were many progenitors to my forceful insistence on integrating cooperative principles into the digital economy.

Prior to our conference, Marjorie Kelly, an author and business ethicist, had been advocating for the adoption of "generative ownership" models for three years.[18] As Schneider was exploring how to transform Uber into a cooperative, Kelly's call for a "reinvention at the level of organizational purpose and structure" resonated deeply with many in the emerging platform co-op movement. People in the movement also drew inspiration from early mentions of cooperative digital platforms in Spain in 2011, demands for a cooperative data commons in Italy in 2012, the establishment of the cooperative marketplace Fairmondo in Germany in the same year, and the launch of Stocksy United, a stock photography and video platform co-op, a year later.

A Movement

"Platform co-ops" as a terminology or concept may, over time, fade into the background of this movement's wider lexicon because of the widespread use and loss of novelty. Nonetheless, this language was and is significant because it serves as a common reference point. Groups that establish "platform co-ops" join a community of founders and members who create novel cooperatives that aren't mere "social enterprises" but are a part of a loosely knit global coalition of cooperatives that operate primarily online.

Platform cooperativism remains an unfinished experiment, a movement that firmly embraces cooperative identity, despite the occasional case of "co-op washing," where deceitful data co-ops or decentralized autonomous organizations pose as genuine cooperatives. "Platform co-op" is not a single model; rather, it encompasses a range of dynamic business models that are continually reevaluated and adjusted over time. The platform co-op movement encourages the integration of shared rituals, music (i.e., an anthem available in several languages), and celebratory events (an annual conference) as an integral part of its ethos, reflecting

Roland Barthes's concept of myth-making. It offers a counter-narrative to the stories coming out of Silicon Valley. Rituals and events are an essential part of platform cooperativism's mythos, inspiring and motivating cooperators to build a more equitable digital economy. It begins with references to utopian socialists such as Robert Owen, whose ideas of alternatives to capitalism inspired the founding of the first worker cooperatives. In addition to Owen, the platform cooperativism movement draws inspiration from historical figures such as Charles Fourier, Henri de Saint-Simon, Pierre-Joseph Proudhon, and John Stuart Mill, who advocated for cooperation and profit-sharing among the working class. William Thompson was also a champion of cooperativism, opposing the concept of competition and calling for a "community of mutual cooperation" capable of establishing islands of suste-nance and production.

People in the platform cooperativism movement draw on a global range of diverse histories and intellectual agendas, includ-ing Robert Owen, a pioneer of cooperative principles. Some find inspiration in E. F. Schumacher's *Small Is Beautiful* or Frederic Laloux's book *Reinventing Organizations*, exploring new organiza-tional paradigms. Others are influenced by Charles Eisenstein's *Sacred Economics*, which calls for a new economic system rooted in the gift economy. Many supporters also acknowledge the princi-ples of Catholic distributism, often associated with G. K. Chesterton, advocating for decentralized ownership to challenge capitalist monopolies and socialism.

The practices of other allies and champions are guided by authors such as Paul Singer, Gustavo Esteva, Noam Chomsky, W. E. B. Du Bois, and Jessica Gordon Nembhard. Their ideas drive supporters to reclaim Indigenous knowledge, encourage worker self-management, amplify economic and racial justice through cooperatives, and support democratic control in the workplace.

This Book

Own This! is about the unfinished story of cooperative principles in the digital economy unfolding through the people who are championing this movement, practicing this culture, advancing this emerging area of academic study, and building this ecosystem of businesses. And although I am the author of this book, the work of many collectives outside of its pages has shaped its creation. I couldn't have written this book without the contributions of co-op practitioners from countless countries, who generously took a break from their inspiring work to share their methods with me.

In this book, not only do I provide a federation-based scaling strategy for platform co-ops and offer suggestions for support from local policymakers, but I also propose the application of the union co-op model to the digital economy. I explore how to effectively frame the often intangible value that platform co-ops create and present my vision of scaling solidarity through a pluralistic digital commonwealth. The book concludes with an epilogue that provides some more insights for implementation. *Own This!* explores both new and old models to determine whether digital platforms with multi-stakeholder, worker-owned, producer-owned, or data cooperative structures could challenge dominant capitalist power structures and promote social justice, complementing legacy models of mutuals, credit unions, and consumer cooperatives. Ultimately, *Own This!* is about the search for allies. To succeed, the platform cooperativism movement must be an internationalist project that transcends divides based on geography and economic status, aligning with broader political coalitions and social movements. The PCC's collaboration with government agencies, cooperative associations in numerous countries, municipalities, and political parties in the UK, US, Brazil, United Arab Emirates, Indonesia, Argentina, Germany, and three states in

India exemplify the burgeoning momentum of this movement. Without support from legislators, however, achieving our goals will be challenging. Collaboration, cohesion, and resource exchange among groups, from Rochdale to Cape Town, are necessary to instill a sense of belonging and build out a global movement. Platform cooperatives will flourish, yet their vitality depends on our level of commitment, legislative success, unity, global coordination, and care.

2

Worker Ownership for the Digital Economy

The US domestic labor market is widely acknowledged to be predominantly occupied by women. Among them, undocumented workers constitute a significant proportion and bear the brunt of the precarity and low wages that often typify the shadow economy.[1] The division lines of gender and citizenship are especially stark in New York City, where nearly half of all domestic workers are undocumented.

There is, however, a group of thirty Spanish-speaking women from the immigrant communities of Brooklyn who are doing better than their peers—much better, in fact. As worker-owners of a young platform cooperative called Up & Go, they earn $25 per hour, or more than twice the $11 they'd usually earned working independently or for traditional digital platforms.[2] As Cirenia Dominguez, Up & Go Cooperative board member and founder of the co-op Brightly, explained to me, being a co-owner of Up & Go also brings nonmaterial benefits. Being the boss, she told me with pride, has given her a sense of dignity and self-worth, as well as new status with family, neighbors, and clients. "I arrived to New York sixteen years ago," Dominguez reports. "Before I joined the co-op, I was trapped in capitalism. The co-op gave me so much worth. When someone hires me or another cleaner, they get to work with the boss herself."[3]

Araceli Dominguez, another Up & Go worker-owner, said, "Before I was part of Up & Go Cooperative, my life was very different. I didn't know my rights. It was unfair sometimes: The working hours were exploitative and we used to suffer from sexual harassment. But now, we are informed. Now I can save money. I can think of the future."[4]

Dominguez's comments about ownership chimed with sentiments I heard from a calm and kind woman in rural Gujarat, India, who was old enough to remember learning rice farming when India was still a British colony. She also recalled with clarity a program in the 1970s that the Indian government called "the White Revolution." The White Revolution was designed to make India's dairy industry economically self-sustaining, and it achieved this goal through the creation of a national milk grid and cooperatives that empowered, trained, and employed poor farmers. But it was another co-op network that was closest to her heart. Standing near two resting cows under a plum tree, we were admiring the lush grass of the family fields when she pulled me in the direction of a nearby water pipe. She smacked it. "SEWA!" she exclaimed, smiling.

SEWA is a union and a cooperative federation—a group of cooperatives that join forces to achieve mutual goals—that in the mid-2000s helped this woman's family purchase infrastructure and learn how to run their farm. Through cooperative ownership, she and her family were able to build a larger stone house and convert their previous home, which was a cement shack with a rusted roof, into a village disco. In my years researching the contemporary cooperative movement, I have heard many deeply moving accounts of the transformative power of cooperative ownership, expressed in different ways by recyclers in São Paulo, care workers in Manchester, seamstresses in Cape Town, farmers near Trivandrum, taxi drivers in Manhattan, and food delivery couriers in Barcelona. As worker-run platforms take root around the world, it can be difficult to keep up with their progress, not to mention their bounty of lessons and insights about how to grow the movement. But one thing is certain. Regardless of whether a worker co-op operates a digital platform or a brick-and-mortar business, is located near the Arabian Sea coast or the Q train in south Brooklyn, its purpose remains the same: to benefit its workers, who often occupy the lowest economic rungs of society, as well as its consumers and communities. Not only do these co-ops put more money into workers' pockets, give them control over their daily schedules, and increase financial and algorithmic transparency, but they also help overcome emotional challenges on the job. As noted by the team of Up & Go, there are important social and psychological benefits. The co-op "isn't only work," said Dominguez. "It is a sisterhood."

This chapter primarily centers on examples of user and worker cooperatives, which, along with multi-stakeholder cooperatives, constitute two principal types of cooperatives classified by the distribution of membership power. Adapting user and worker co-op models in the creation of tech start-ups can promote equitable distribution of ownership and control, democratic decision-making, and support for workers' rights and well-being in the digital economy.

The emergence of distributed technologies associated with blockchains, crypto, and "Web3," along with the rise of decentralized autonomous organizations (DAOs), provides a unique opportunity to re-envision traditional cooperatives and the way tech start-ups function. These technologies not only inspire a new wave of cooperatives but also encourage tech collectives to explore and experiment with cooperative principles. Indeed, in response to all these developments, the International Cooperative Alliance—with roots dating back to 1895 as a global organization that promotes cooperative ideals, principles, and unity—may be compelled to reconsider its seven cooperative guiding principles in order to accommodate these realities.

The International Cooperative Alliance (ICA), is a pivotal player in shaping the digital future of the cooperative movement. As traditional manufacturing declines and labor markets on the internet grow, the ICA must boldly embrace technological transformation. As a global steward for cooperatives, the ICA can actively promote and support experiments aimed at establishing the cooperative identity in the digital economy. This includes negotiating data standards for a worldwide cooperative data commons, starting perhaps in the agriculture sector.

The efforts of the ICA are particularly vital and necessary, given the reluctance of traditional enterprises to meaningfully help democratize the internet. Despite the endeavors of proponents of "enlightened capitalism," traditional entities have proven ill-equipped and unwilling to meaningfully democratize the public corporation. In this chapter, I will elaborate on my skepticism toward the notion that major technology companies can be compelled into making significant strides in the direction of workplace fairness, economic justice, and democratic power sharing. By holding up a mirror to profit-maximizing business models, I will illustrate how cooperative ownership can serve as a catalyst for a people's economy.

The Pandemic's Reality Check on Stakeholder Capitalism

A few years ago, the Business Roundtable, a gathering of two hundred chief executives from the world's largest corporations, including Walmart, JPMorgan, and Amazon, decided to advocate for something called "stakeholder capitalism." This new capitalism was meant to be more enlightened and broadly distributive than the old capitalism, which was driven by a narrow philosophy of maximizing shareholder value. The executives pledged to lead their firms for the "benefit of all stakeholders: consumers, employees, suppliers, communities, and shareholders."[5] The chairman of Salesforce even declared capitalism as we knew it to be "dead."[6] Moving forward, corporate America would organize itself in a more democratic and stakeholder-focused manner. People in the audience seemed impressed. "Let's give them the benefit of our doubt," I heard one US government official say as we exited the auditorium.

A few years later, when the pandemic struck, this "transformation" was put to a test and utterly failed. Corporations that had so recently proclaimed their rejection of shareholder capitalism predictably turned against their workers. The founder of Amazon raised prices on essential products by as much as 1,000 percent and denied hazard and sick pay to over 450,000 Amazon employees. His personal fortune, meanwhile, increased by $97 billion. Shareholders rejoiced. The other "stakeholders," not so much.

It is not just that CEOs broke their promises. The pandemic revealed the extent to which the public corporation is bound by the dominant logic of profit maximization, regardless of what executives say in front of the media.

As a matter of fact, the topic of alternative business models has not gone away; it continues to be a burning issue. The arenas of conflict extend from Amazon union drives to large labor platform companies such as Lyft, which are facing legal challenges over the categories of employment that determine the extent of their drivers' protection under established labor law. Trading work for a traditional monolithic corporation with work for a monopolistic platform may not be the best option for individuals or society.

Not surprisingly, the large tech companies that shape our digital economy are actively lobbying against measures that would grant platform-economy workers labor rights. These companies, often relying solely on investor contributions, use their funds to exert influence over regulators and grant unelected elites increased political control. The impact of monopolies extends beyond their own industry, having detrimental effects on other sectors as well. In 2020, a coalition of tech companies, including Uber, Lyft, DoorDash, Instacart, and others, spent more than $200 million pushing for California Proposition 22 as a way to avoid providing benefits and protections to workers who would otherwise be classified as employees in the state.[7] Proposition 22 was later passed by voters.

These companies do not always have a problem with activist government, of course. Google is actively lobbying for regulation that would grant it more influence over the educational content available to children. In the meantime, Uber is backing legislation that could enable the company to actively challenge public transportation, including buses, subways, and trams.

Pharmaceutical companies, such as Johnson & Johnson and Pfizer, promote addictive drugs to expand their customer base, as demonstrated by the opioid crisis, with Johnson & Johnson found guilty of deceptive and dangerous marketing campaigns that significantly increased addiction and overdose deaths, and Pfizer paying a $2.2 billion fine to settle federal charges of illegal drug marketing.[8]

Control over industries extends beyond software and drugs, with even the food we consume falling prey to monopolies. In the United States, just three processors—Tyson, Pilgrim's Pride, and Perdue—dominate the chicken market. For many farmers, selling their chickens to a single buyer is the only option, and dissenting from the buyer's terms can result in financial ruin.

All this raises a critical question: Do we condone granting control of vital aspects of our lives, such as health care, food supply, transportation systems, and education, to a handful of corporations? The resounding answer is no, which compels us to ensure that tech giants are held accountable to antitrust regulations, and to recognize cooperatives as a viable antidote to counteract monopoly power as part of a comprehensive anti-trust agenda.

The dominance of a few big tech companies is an expression of the deepening concentration of corporate ownership, with Black-Rock, Vanguard, and State Street being the dominant shareholders in 88 percent of the 500 largest US-listed firms, and 40 percent of all publicly traded US companies, making them de facto owners with voting rights that they consistently use to vote in favor of management and against shareholder proposals.[9] While shareholder capitalism was intended to promote market democratization and investment, today's markets fall short of democratic principles. Mere lip service and hollow assurances from corporate leaders are woefully inadequate. What we need is a radical reimagining of our economic system that prioritizes equity, justice, and sustainability as a matter of urgency.

To begin, how did we get to this point of concentrated ownership of the internet's most critical components? At first, the internet was hailed as a space with unlimited potential, a level playing field where anybody could freely share their ideas and even live their wildest libertarian fantasies, free of corporate gatekeepers. Anything seemed possible. But the internet's original idealistic vision of a democratized and decentralized space has given way to a highly commercialized and centralized environment.

This evolution of the internet was not inevitable, nor was it the consequence of a transhistorical fact about technical advancement; rather, it was the product of decisions taken by legislators and business leaders. Amid growing public frustration and anger over the reign of "absentee shareholders" who are disconnected from communities and the manipulation of users, exemplified by scandals such as Facebook–Cambridge Analytica's data scraping of 80 million individuals, there is still hope to reclaim the internet as a public good, foster a more democratic digital commons, and create an online environment that upholds its original promise and promotes community ownership.

The pandemic has led to a staggering 85 percent of workers around the world feeling disengaged and discontent with their jobs, as many have left big companies in droves.[10] The average platform worker faces isolation and physical risks as they earn barely enough to subsist, trapped in a toxic mix of underpayment and technologically enhanced monitoring.

From nineteenth-century Utopian Socialists like Robert Owen to contemporary voices like American linguist, philosopher, and social critic Noam Chomsky, thinkers have theorized how to best "appropriate the appropriators," on the level of the state, smaller social units, workplaces, and all the way down to the individual. The cooperative ownership model, inspired by Henri Saint-Simon, Charles Fourier, and Owens, promotes the long-term health of the business and worker co-ownership, restoring dignity and control. It allows individuals to work with trusted friends locally while participating in a global digital platform, and gives people control over their personal data. In recent years, this model has gained traction in a variety of sectors, from renewable energy co-ops to ride-sharing platforms, and from agencies of interpreters to online bookstores. Cooperative ownership differs from "absentee shareholders" in that it connects workers as true stakeholders, according to the American philosopher Robert Edward Freeman's stakeholder theory. This theory posits a "community of interests" that connects each business not just to shareholders but also to workers, consumers, suppliers, small investors, and the broader community, with its diverse concerns and interests. In the co-op model, the community of workers and users is the lifeblood of the operation.

The Complexity of Ownership Models

Cooperatives, much like interconnected archipelagos with distinct local habitats, emerge in an infinite variety of shapes and sizes, influenced by local languages, economic conditions, cultural traditions, and political landscapes. This diversity makes it challenging to discuss them as a homogeneous force. Patrons run the Park Slope Food Coop in Brooklyn and Florida's Natural Growers through membership votes or other means, while other cooperatives may take the form of community-owned wind turbines or sports teams such as the Green Bay Packers or FC Barcelona, with fans and supporters as collective team owners.[11]

Cooperative ownership is one form of employee ownership, with another common form being employee stock ownership plans (ESOPs), which distribute company stock to employees via a US trust structure. ESOPs, the most common form of employee ownership in the United States, are a popular choice with the current count at approximately 6,500.[12] ESOPs distribute company stock to employees without typically giving them much say in how the company is run. They are ideologically diverse and highly complex.

Despite some ESOPs having been associated with fraudulent behavior and poor working conditions, there is evidence that many ESOPs successfully foster positive work environments, with some being recognized in "Great Place to Work" studies. For instance, the Chinese technology firm Huawei paid $9.65 billion in dividends to current and retired employees in 2022, demonstrating the potential for ESOPs to financially benefit workers.[13] To be fair, some cooperatives, especially larger ones, also produce mixed results, and have strayed from cooperative principles over time.

During the COVID-19 pandemic, European proposals to nationalize Amazon popularized a direct path to public ownership, which is another ownership model for addressing community needs. Nationalizing major social media companies such as Facebook has also been frequently discussed in European capitals, including Brussels. The model of major television or radio stations being state-owned and -run is one that Germans, for instance, are intimately acquainted with. Despite intense debates about public television services such as ARD and ZDF in Germany, they are widely acknowledged to serve the public interest by promoting education and healthier lifestyles. It's not surprising, then, that many Germans are receptive to the idea of major social media platforms that are either user-owned or run and owned by the state. In contrast, because of the broadly perceived dysfunction of the US government, many Americans remain skeptical about the prospect of federal ownership of the platform through which they express their thoughts and feelings.

Critics of nationalization do have a considerable amount of history on their side, especially cooperators who may be skeptical of dreams of nationalization; they may remember that since the early 1840s, when the first recognizable cooperatives were formed, government bureaucrats, colonial rule, and later socialist governments have frequently compromised their overall purpose, often using the cooperative form to promote their own political and economic agendas. Outright nationalization (and expropriation) is further complicated by the sensitive nature of businesses that deal with personal data, free speech, and other areas ripe for abuse.

There is also the matter of overcoming the fierce resistance of current stakeholders. This was on display in May 2017, when Nathan Schneider helped bring a grassroots proposal to Twitter's annual shareholders' meeting that invited the then-struggling company to investigate the possibility of user ownership. At the time, Twitter wasn't exactly a cash cow, failing to churn out the frenzied profits and growth rates that the VCs and investors had been salivating for. And that's when the perfect chance presented itself to unleash a novel ownership approach that would disentangle the platform from the myopic financial motives of its private shareholders.

"Wall Street's economy has become Twitter's economy," said Schneider in an interview. "But Wall Street's view of the platform's usefulness isn't necessarily our view. What if we changed Twitter's economy? What if users were to band together and buy Twitter for themselves?"

The proposed user-led buyout, as crafted with the help of early Twitter investor Armin Steuernagel, called for the creation of a joint-equity company to crowdfund the 20 percent of cash needed to buy a majority stake in the platform. Once the platform was under user ownership, voting rights would be distributed according to the value contributed to the network, privileging Twitter's staff and its most active users.

Schneider contends that in conjunction with regulation, user ownership can provide a mechanism for ensuring democratic self-governance and equitable profit sharing within digital platforms. Building on the experience of ESOPs, he argues for the creation of user-trusts to facilitate the transition to the user–owner model.

In addition to options like ESOPs, co-ops, and public ownership, the history of workers purchasing financially struggling companies is long and storied, especially when such purchases involve the recuperation of the factories in which they worked. And these examples are not confined to the past. Following the late-1990s financial crisis that saw the collapse of the Argentinian peso in 2001, more than 300 factories were "recovered" by Argentinian workers. In the United States, workers at a Chicago-based window company occupied their foreclosed factory and turned it into a worker-owned cooperative, New Era Windows, in 2012.

But the scale and complexity of a global social media giant makes it challenging to envision worker recuperation working in the same way as it has for start-ups and abandoned factories.

Twitter's board of directors and major investors—the latter expecting a unicorn payout, at least—were opposed to the idea of a user buyout. Converting Twitter's ownership structure to user ownership has the potential to address the concerns about data surveillance and unaccountable platform ownership. However, ensuring meaningful democratic decision-making with Twitter's large user base raises feasibility questions. The possibility of sound decisions and upholding integrity through alternative decision-making structures, such as user assemblies, remains uncertain and may risk an emotionally charged "tyranny of the majority."

We cannot know the answers to these questions until we try, but one thing is clear: The Twitter acquisition by Elon Musk underscores the need for democratic oversight of influential digital platforms. Creating smaller, cooperatively owned alternatives to Twitter is a more feasible short-term goal than attempting to take over a massive social platform. Such platforms could promote genuine community connection much along the lines of what Howard Rheingold described as "virtual community."

While many scholars have proposed approaches to regulating and transforming digital platforms, British political scientist James Muldoon introduces the concept of social ownership in his book *Platform Socialism*. Muldoon advocates for "organizing the digital economy through social ownership of digital assets and democratic control over the infrastructure and systems that govern our digital lives," which includes a combination of state ownership and other ownership models. Muldoon believes that the "municipal movement" is a key driver for achieving this goal, as municipalities are ideal sites for experimentation and ways in which citizens can regain power.

One of this movement's central demands is for power to be decentralized and devolved away from the nation state and toward local governments, which can better respond to the specific needs of their citizens. Citing examples from Rosario in Argentina, London, Barcelona, and San Francisco, Muldoon argues that allied municipalities are best suited to assisting nascent platform cooperatives and moving society as a whole toward systemic platform socialism.

In a co-authored policy paper titled "Policies for Cooperative Ownership in the Digital Economy" published in 2022, I echoed Muldoon's approach in emphasizing the role of municipal policies in promoting cooperative ownership. The paper argued that cooperatives could, for instance, accept noncontrolling shares from municipalities, making local governments nonvoting members that participate in the co-op's operations without controlling them.[14] We understood this as a way to provide financial support and strengthen their connection with the local community.

The cooperative model is well suited to strengthening marginalized people. We heard about SEWA's 300,000-member cooperative federation in India that provides an example of how cooperative models can empower marginalized communities: Women who were previously considered untouchables can now engage in a shared life project, make decisions together, and live in dignity, even in a toxic patriarchal environment. They can improve their lives now, as they don't have to wait for scholars' imagined futures, such as a post-work society, post-capitalism, and eco-socialism (as valid, needed, and important as they are), to become a reality; they can participate now in entry points that lead to those better worlds, flawed as they may be.

Among proponents of the different ownership models I introduced, there is often intense and sometimes almost faith-based rivalry. Success, however, requires embracing a diversity of approaches rather than rigidly adhering to a single perspective or point of view. This requires a wide range of skill sets, including business and technology expertise, community building, cultural shaping, policy research, global coordination, and public advocacy, as well as both symbolic and practical actions. What matters most is that we foster an atmosphere of mutual support and cooperation rooted in the conviction that we are all working toward shared goals. Instead of perpetuating circular firing squads, let us break free and joyfully trip the light fantastic, moving to the tunes of solidarity.

To understand the power of cooperative ownership models, we can look to the United States, where over 650,000 people are released from prison each year, and worker cooperatives offer a chance for some of them to live dignified lives and make decisions together. Tightshift Laboring Cooperative, a worker-owned business co-op in Washington, DC, for example, is offering employment and healing opportunities for formerly incarcerated people. The co-op offers manual labor services and uses eco-friendly products to provide affordable, high-quality cleaning services. Core Staffing, a cooperative staffing agency for return-ing citizens in Baltimore, is another example. Worker cooperatives not only provide stable employment for formerly incarcerated individuals but also offer them an opportunity to have a meaning-ful say in decisions that affect their lives and communities. This is particularly important since many of these individuals are routinely disadvantaged and denied the right to vote in federal elections. As cooperatives are owned and governed by their mem-bers, each member, regardless of their background, has an equal say, allowing returning citizens to reclaim a sense of voice, owner-ship, and autonomy in their workplace.

Why then, despite the fact that worker-owned platform coop-eratives have the potential to create substantial social value, is their prevalence in the emerging digital economy still relatively limited? Part of this has to do with a lack of awareness. Despite their long history and strong presence in low- and high-income countries, cooperatives aren't taught in law schools or listed as an option in business schools.[15] The reason they are not even included in economics textbooks is due to the dominance of mainstream economic paradigms upheld by scholars, biased narratives favoring private ownership, limited awareness, corporate influence, shortage of research, and perception challenges surrounding cooperatives.

According to the theory of hegemonic common sense proposed by Italian philosopher Antonio Gramsci, the dominant culture maintains the status quo by using culture as a weapon, often in myriad and subtle ways. We take conventional corporations and employment relations for granted, as something as natural as the air we breathe, and are taught to applaud charitable foundations when they place low-income immigrants or other disadvantaged groups in low-level corporate jobs. But assisting them to own and run businesses? This is simply not yet part of the desirable spectrum of choices. One foundation has labeled the worker-owned Up & Go "un-American," while several students from well-respected universities have reported that their professors reflexively oppose the cooperative ownership model and frequently prefer to portray cooperatives as principled, well-meaning institutions that struggle with funding and governance issues and will never be able to scale effectively. Shifting this Overton window will require serious work, education, and time.[16]

Cooperative ownership has been described as "the exercise of a bundle of rights [that] makes the firm exist as a collective entity beyond its individual members."[17] The patronage activity in cooperatives often confers rights, but the relationship between ownership and control is often misconstrued. To begin, many people believe that "ownership" means having complete control over a company's operating rules and money flows, ideally without having to participate in governance structures. This is how things work within the modern corporation, where money buys influence and power, but such ownership is out of reach for the average American wage earner. But the worker-owned cooperative offers a different, democratic kind of power, in which all member-owners enjoy equal standing. In this case, influence must be earned. In hierarchical or merit-based systems, decisions are often made without input from all members. However, in participatory worker cooperatives, decisions are made democratically, with members persuading their colleagues to support their ideas. Factors such as charisma, cultural homogeneity, and friendships can influence the success of this process. While formal equality in cooperatives is not threatened by money, the model does not guarantee fair outcomes. Nevertheless, democratic arrangements in cooperatives rooted in a strong social purpose increase the likelihood of achieving fair and participatory outcomes.

Coding Values: The Case of Up & Go

Up & Go, the platform for home cleaning services in New York City, exemplifies how cooperative ownership can create a more equitable wealth distribution in a digital platform economy. As a member of one of the 465 mostly for-profit worker cooperatives in the United States, Up & Go's women have discovered four salient features to operating their platform co-op, which offer a stark contrast to the challenges and frustrations that come with launching a conventional tech start-up: visibility for otherwise precarious small co-ops; access to more work and higher income; a streamlined booking process; and the opportunity to attract more co-op members.

As in other co-ops, Up & Go's salary bands and market rates are not used to determine the pay of CEO-level employees. Instead, pay is determined like every other issue: democratically. This brings with it psychological and social benefits that are difficult to quantify. "A traditional business can make you feel bad about yourself at work," one Up & Go worker told me.

"That's not the case when you work in a cooperative. You own the business and get paid for it. If you own something, you own your work."[18]

The challenge of balancing personal desires with the needs of the business has been integral to the organizational culture of worker cooperatives since their inception. For two centuries, worker-owners have been confronted with this tension but continue to tackle it through democratic processes, while striving to find solutions that support both the success of the business and the well-being of its members.[19]

Up & Go is an umbrella co-op uniting three independent worker co-ops run by female, mostly Latina, immigrant workers in Brooklyn. The organization functions a bit like a guild, in that it controls and guarantees labor supply, establishes its own rules, and provides professional development support. Each of Up & Go's worker co-ops—Brightly, EcoMundo, and Cooperative Cleaning—is legally registered as an LLC, a type of business easily established in the United States.

As I mentioned at the outset of this chapter, women make up the majority of all maids, cleaners, and nannies in New York's domestic work sector; half are undocumented.[20] In New York City alone, the residential cleaning market is $273 million-a-year strong. The cooperative home cleaning market is just a small slice of that, at $1.5 million.[21] But "the benefits of owning your own business are immense and diverse—including the opportunity to own something without employment papers," says Michael Paone, a project coordinator for policy, advocacy, and research at the Federation of Protestant Welfare Agencies.[22] In so many ways, the Up & Go women are following in the footsteps of African Americans, who have a long history of cooperative ownership, "particularly as part of an economic development strategy and a larger economic independence movement," as American scholar Jessica Gordon Nembhard emphasizes in her book *Collective Courage*.[23]

As co-owners, the women of Up & Go are compelled to make critical decisions about the platform's features and overall operation. Each has one vote regardless of seniority. Since Up & Go eliminates the intermediary, it charges a tiny 5 percent commission, with 95 percent of revenues going directly to the co-ops. Compare this with traditional tech platforms that routinely take a hefty 20 to 50 percent cut out of workers' paychecks.

It's not surprising that conventional companies, which do not prioritize worker ownership as a core value, are often less productive than companies like Up & Go that do prioritize worker ownership. American scholar Richard Freeman cites statistical evidence that "firms in which workers have a property stake [such as Up & Go] are more productive, induce more worker effort and responsibility, spur workers to innovate more, and produce diverse other benefits for workers."[24] Up & Go's workers collectively own 100 percent of the business; there are no outside stakes. In 2022, members voted to implement an annual membership fee of approximately $75 per person, but ownership does not require the purchase of shares. Up & Go not only prevents customers from requesting a specific worker for their subsequent appointments, thereby reducing the risk of sexual harassment, but also ensures the use of nontoxic and eco-friendly cleaning chemicals.

Worker cooperatives provide an important alternative to the systemic racism they may face elsewhere and that continues to degrade Black and brown working-class people in the United States. By embracing cooperative ownership models, both traditional and digital platforms, people can work toward building a more equitable and just society. Cooperative ownership is a compelling prospect for low-income minorities to sidestep the exclusion and marginalization that permeate mainstream economic structures and institutions. By embracing cooperative ownership, they may control their economic destinies and become the builders of their own workplaces. In worker cooperatives, members are able to work together as equals, while retaining control over crucial decision-making aspects of the business, such as product and service design, compensation structures, and data governance policies. These are not abstract notions but lived experiences. This is important, says Esteban Kelly, director of the United States Federation of Worker Cooperatives, because the tangible benefits of ownership—such as the power to liquidate or leverage an asset to obtain needed funds—complement appealing but abstract concepts such as dignity and solidarity.

Cooperative values are coded into these institutions. In the case of digital platform cooperatives, they are literally coded. When CoLab, an upstate New York–based tech cooperative, collaborated with Up & Go worker-owners to design their mobile-friendly website and phone app, they followed the workers' wish to omit individual worker profiles. This matters as labor platforms, as described by social psychologist Shoshana Zuboff, are a new form of behavioral modification, exemplified through the use of opaque algorithms that are effectively meant to replace human bosses for taxi drivers and food delivery couriers.[25] Beyond this, built-in reputation systems in VC-backed apps often pit workers against each other, leading to firings for low scores. The members of Up & Go have a say in the platform's coding to ensure that it aligns with their values. They also hired CoLab, a culturally compatible tech cooperative to do the coding work, which allows the worker-owners to keep the intellectual property rights over the software that powers the Up & Go website. They've never had any kind of copyright ownership or control over their technology, and doing so provides them with a sense of agency and control. Each woman embodies not only a contract worker but also a business owner and tech entrepreneur.

Not every co-op supporter is a fan of the fact that the Up & Go website was not open source from the get-go. Although CoLab advocates for open source, and the women of Up & Go did not hold any ideological stance against it, Up & Go's primary focus on the survival of their business meant that open source was simply not a priority for them in the beginning. Nevertheless, they are now exploring licensing models and actively contemplating how to make their source code more accessible. A pro-commons approach, where open source or source-available code is adopted as a fundamental aspect of platform co-op ownership, would significantly advance cooperative values and help further movement goals. Additionally, the software used by Up & Go could be shared with other cooperatives in compliance with the International Cooperative Alliance's sixth principle, which promotes cooperation among cooperatives.

As I had noted earlier, traditional VCs, foundations, and municipalities often assume that people from immigrant backgrounds or economically disadvantaged circumstances are incapable of setting up, owning, and operating a tech start-up. Platform co-ops such as Drivers Cooperative and Up & Go demonstrate that with the right assistance, they are. Up & Go partners with the Center for Family Life (CFL). Initially, the CFL focused on providing support to low-income communities lacking basic employment skills, such as résumé preparation, interviewing techniques, and interview dress codes. Recognizing the uphill battle of placing individuals in dignified, higher-paying jobs, however, CFL began supporting the development of cooperatives. CFL's key insight was that traditional employment opportunities for disadvantaged individuals did not provide dignified or well-paying-enough work to sustain a decent living, whereas worker cooperatives offered a viable alternative.

Not only do cooperative developers such as CFL support the establishment of platform cooperatives, but unions also play a role in supporting them. An example is the Barcelona-based delivery platform co-op Mensakas, which received software assistance from CoopCycle, a French shared-services cooperative, and governance and public education support from Intersindical Alternativa de Catalunya (IAC), a Catalonian trade union association representing six unions with 11,600 members across various sectors.[26]

Data Cooperatives and Other Experiments with Ownership and Governance

So far, this chapter emphasizes the dignity of cooperative ownership by showcasing various examples of successful cooperatives and their potential benefits, such as better wages, retention, long-tern viability, and sustainability; improved working conditions; and a greater sense of community and solidarity among workers. But this story is also of the emergence of data cooperatives, trusts, unions, and DAOs, machine learning, and distributed technologies to develop new governance models for data, prioritizing decentralization, social impact, inclusivity, mutuality, collective governance, and transparency. These models build upon the cooperative model of collective ownership and management, allowing individuals to pool their data for collective benefit and manage that benefit through collective access and control.

MIDATA, a nonprofit data cooperative, is a good example. MIDATA was established in 2015 by researchers from ETH Zurich and Bern University of Applied Sciences. Its mission is to support users by giving them control over their health data, allowing them to decide who can access it and for what purpose. This cooperative model of collective ownership and management ensures that the benefits of health data are shared more equitably among the people who produce it. MIDATA's modular architecture and governance structure enable the formation of sister cooperatives in other regions, allowing for greater scalability and impact while maintaining its commitment to privacy and transparency.

Similarly, polypoly Cooperative, a German data cooperative established four years after MIDATA, enables users to store their data on their own devices, granting them control over their information and exemplifying a collaborative and modular approach to data governance. Where data cooperatives provide individuals with access and control in organizations that collect and use data, DAOs enable collective decision-making without intermediaries or centralized authority, allowing for decentralized and self-governed communities to operate transparently. DAOs aim to establish trust through hard-coded rules, distributing ownership through tokens and allowing voting rights based on stakeholder ownership, patronage, or reputation. The models of governance mandated by DAOs, combined with cooperative ownership and management, have the potential to shift power from platforms to their users, and have already made initial legislative inroads in the EU. Beyond DAOs, data cooperatives, user trusts, and data unions can use AI, machine learning, and distributed technologies to develop new governance models for data.

The stories presented illustrate how cooperative ownership can promote greater control, equity, and justice in multiple sectors and contexts, ultimately contributing to a greater sense of well-being for workers, communities, and individuals. Worker cooperatives and platform worker cooperatives can be a critical safety net and a lifeline for those who are on the fringes of society.

When I recall the elderly lady in Gujarat proudly placing her hand on the water pipe that rescued her family from poverty, I am reminded of so many others I've met with who can tell similar stories: the food couriers racing through Barcelona, Berlin, and Bologna, and the New York City taxi drivers and housekeepers whose lives have been uplifted through cooperatives. I envision a scenario where we all gather together, where skeptics, including economics professors, mayors, and foundation officers who flatly repudiated all forms of employee ownership, sit alongside the workers whose lives have been transformed. In the stories of care workers and taxi drivers, we see profound life transformations through cooperative ownership, acknowledging that worker cooperatives have effectively turned their lives around. I hope that skeptics of these models will be persuaded by the clear-cut evidence, prompting them to reevaluate and understand the urgency of supplying the financial, institutional, and political support needed for its realization across the face of a planet in crisis.

3

Solidarity at Scale

In the summer of 2018, I traveled to the bustling western Indian city of Ahmedabad, a cotton and textiles capital of more than 8 million people on the banks of the Sabarmati River. My contact and guide in the city was Namya Mahajan, the thirty-year-old managing director of the Self-Employed Women's Association (SEWA), a union and national federation of 106 cooperatives headquartered in a simple three-story red-brick building close to the Sabarmati Ashram, where Mahatma Gandhi lived when he was not traveling or imprisoned.

Since its founding in 1972 by a group of local women seeking microloans for their businesses, SEWA has expanded to become a federation of cooperatives with a presence in a range of traditional and modern industries, from milk production to pharmaceuticals to garment manufacturing. For five decades, it has been more than a national force in India: it has performed as a global beacon, the largest organization of women in informal work arrangements in the world.

The association's culture reflects the multireligious texture of its membership. On my first morning in Ahmedabad, I joined Namya and a group of twenty-five women on a traditional hand-woven crimson-and-blue-patterned carpet that stretched across the large community room at Lok Swasthya SEWA Trust, SEWA's national headquarters. It is here that the staff begins each day with unsectarian chants that acknowledge the rich tapestry of spiritual life on the subcontinent. Hindu, Muslim, Jain, Christian, nondenominational—the musical odes constitute an expansive, inclusive ritual.

Over the decades, SEWA's mission and activities have grown to mirror this expansiveness. Since its founding half a century ago to help impoverished women obtain capital, the organization has evolved into a multifaceted operation that not only supports women-run cooperatives but also helps members develop as leaders and strengthen cooperative governance practices. It offers a sweeping range of social services to families, including literacy, nutritional counseling, and childcare. This holistic-ecosystem approach, which addresses both social and economic needs, is critical to SEWA's success in meeting the needs of poor women workers in India's dominant informal economy.

The seed of this model was present from the start. The group's founder, the late Ela Ramesh Bhatt, a Gandhian activist and organizer, incorporated literacy programs into her efforts to help women classified as "unbankable" by the nationalized state banks at the time. The skills the women gained allowed them to achieve something remarkable: SEWA established Shri Mahila Sewa Sahakari Bank, Ltd—SEWA Bank for short—in 1974 with a capital contribution of 100,000 rupees (about $12,440 at the time). Four thousand women made contributions as small as ten rupees (about twelve cents at the time of writing this).

The women soon realized that the high cost of medical expenses in India made it difficult or impossible for many of the bank's members to repay their microloans. They then set about creating a program, launched in 1984, to offer health insurance to their members at a cost of 85 rupees per year. Around the same time, SEWA began expanding beyond its urban roots, fanning out to the countryside to help women develop rural and agricultural cooperatives. In a word, SEWA had begun to scale.

Within the cooperative movement, the concept of "scaling" stirs passionate discussions and remains one of the most conceptually contentious terms due to its intricate intellectual lineage and the challenge of preserving cooperative culture and ensuring transparency.

In particular, it owes its enduring influence to the 1973 bestseller *Small Is Beautiful: A Study of Economics as if People Mattered*, by the British-German economist E. F. Schumacher.[1] Inspired by his travels in Burma, Schumacher firmly believed that small companies are often the most suitable choice. In place of economic "giantism," so characteristic of the 1970s, he proposed a green, human-scale approach to economics and technology generally. The modern Schumacherian critique often reflects ideas drawn from a number of faith traditions, but none of these traditions, not even Buddhism, expressly opposes scaling. It is possible to believe in the value of both small- and large-scale platform co-ops while adhering to their core teachings. As I hope to show in this chapter, gaining an understanding of scaling in a platform cooperative involves considering various factors and complexities. It is crucial to acknowledge that there is no one-size-fits-all solution, as the optimal size depends on the unique characteristics of the business, sector, and location, spanning from local to global. Platform cooperatives achieve scaling through strategies such as federation and shared digital infrastructure, transitioning start-ups to community ownership, exploring Web3 prototypes and establishing global cooperatives, and while also considering factors such as conducive regulation, legal structures, and cooperative development institutions.

The ambiguity surrounding scaling poses a challenge, as some oppose any form of growth, even if it promotes climate tech solutions or generates employment opportunities for the previously unemployed.

Sectors such as ride-hailing or short-term rentals may demand international expansion, while areas such as home services or care can flourish without becoming global digital platforms. Recognizing the unlikely prospect of achieving the growth trajectory of Silicon Valley tech firms in these sectors, I embrace the concept of "nonscalability" proposed by anthropologist Anna Lowenhaupt Tsing in "On Nonscalability: The Living World Is Not Amenable to Precision-Nested Scales," particularly in contexts such as home care and domestic work, where the intricacies of the natural world resist rigid hierarchical scales. How we define this process of scaling and its objectives determines whether we can hold constructive conversations about when and how scaling is expedient or meaningful, both for a particular co-op or for the movement as a whole. Any discussion of scaling must begin with a clear statement of what scaling is not. It is not the thing we are working against; that is, it is not a mirror of venture capital logic, which prioritizes growth for its own sake as a source of increased investment and profit, and maximizes the economic interests of operators.[2] This should be clear from the historical record of the movement. In roughly two centuries, has there ever been an instance of a worker cooperative founded with the goal of obliterating a global monopoly in the manner of traditional economic actors?

I believe it is a mistake to use the term "scaling" as shorthand for expansion in pursuit of market dominance. Scaling does not even require that a business strive to operate in as many localities and countries as possible, or reach the greatest number of customers. The key metric for cooperative scaling is very different: the most crucial factor is getting the best possible overall outcome/return, which is distinct from ordinary financial returns. There is the broad "social return," which includes both financial profit and social benefit. According to economists, this is the financial profit after accounting for both positive and negative "externalities." Cooperatives operate in a political and economic environment where they bear the burden of external costs, considering negative environmental and social impacts as part of their business model and decision-making processes, while traditional firms are not usually required to take full responsibility for these impacts.

To this end, distinctions must be drawn not only between the values and goals of traditional and cooperative scaling, but also between *types* of cooperative scaling.

The first type of cooperative scaling is "scaling up." This superficially resembles traditional scaling, since it involves an increase in the size of an operation and its economies of scale. But as we will see, it serves a very different purpose in a cooperative context. Second, there is "scaling out," which refers to the seeding and replication of models and similar activity in other territories and sectors. Finally, "scaling deep" involves creating value in a specific location through mindful, culturally aware, participatory practices that prioritize care and the deepening of relationships among stakeholders.[3]

Economists debate scale versus scope, as well as the differences between vertical, horizontal, and conglomerate scale. "Scale" refers to the size of a company; "scope" refers to the breadth of its operations. Vertical scaling occurs when a company expands its operations inside a particular industry. A small bakery that sells only bread may decide, for instance, to start offering sandwiches and pastries as well. Horizontal scaling occurs when a firm expands its activities into other industries. A garment company, for example, might start selling household goods, or a technology company might start selling automobiles. Conglomerate scale develops when one company buys another in a different industry. For example, a pharmaceutical company might acquire a chain of retail stores, or a media company might take over a construction company.

The popular discussion around the scaling of platform co-ops often focuses unhelpfully on a narrow understanding of "scaling up." Many scholars have approached the debate about scaling platform cooperatives by examining their potential to defeat titans of industry such as Google or Uber, ultimately concluding that they are unlikely to do so. This framing, however, yields the right answer to the wrong question. Cooperatives have rarely put corporations out of business in the past, and this monopoly-minded framing obfuscates both the reasons why most social justice–leaning cooperatives have not scaled effectively and the goals for which scaling can be used to advance cooperative goals and values.

The outward and deep scaling of SEWA shows that cooperative scaling is not the scaling sought by Silicon Valley start-ups. It is also an object lesson in how growth need not be the enemy of cooperative success or ideals. It demonstrates how scaling can be achieved through alliances and federations that replicate successful local and translocal models and act as force multipliers for their members and social goals. This kind of scaling follows what I call a *systems* or *ecosystem approach*, one that seeks to build up a network of institutions working toward a shared vision.

As we will explore, certain sectors are particularly conducive to the development of a cooperative ecosystem or confederation in which platform cooperatives thrive and collaborate. This model represents a digital upgrade of the global confederation of cooperatives espoused by nineteenth-century utopian socialists and unions such as the American Knights of Labor, whose program in the 1880s called for the creation of a multiracial "cooperative commonwealth."[4]

To reclaim the concept of a cooperative commonwealth in the digital age, it is important to tackle the skepticism among co-op supporters that often stifles meaningful discussions on scaling. For some, the concept of "scaling" is perceived as a Trojan Horse that surreptitiously introduces corporate "growthism," potentially undermining the core principles of cooperatives.

I experienced this firsthand in June 2020 during a series of events and courses hosted by the organization I founded at the

New School, the Platform Cooperativism Consortium, in partnership with Mondragon University. It was on the heels of the first wave of the pandemic and attracted more than a thousand participants from dozens of countries.[5] During my presentation on scaling in the "Platform Co-ops Now!" course, I encountered strong opposition when proposing that the internet could enable cooperative ownership to transcend traditional brick-and-mortar models. Some participants humorously threatened me with "coop purgatory." However, this sparked a wider dialogue about the circumstances that necessitate scaling. We deliberated over the justifiability of rejecting scaling, despite its potential to create numerous better-paying, dignified jobs with collective voice and representation, improved bargaining power in supplier relationships, and positive environmental impact.

In this chapter, one objective is to demonstrate that a pluralistic cooperative economy, comprising interdependent yet autonomous cooperatives, serves a purpose beyond solely challenging the dominant players in the digital economy. While striving to surpass these top-tier players is commendable (and where appropriate, we should!), it is crucial to acknowledge that their ongoing presence should not be perceived as a failure. If Jason S. Spicer's assertion holds true that individual cooperatives "must achieve scale to be sufficiently efficient to survive,"[6] this can be accomplished through federated networks of small, local cooperatives or cooperative conglomerates that leverage shared digital infrastructure, thereby attaining some of the efficiencies associated with larger, more conventional entities. However, it is essential to emphasize that the value of these cooperatives should not be measured by their ability to "slay the Uber dragon."

During the debate over Amazon's ill-fated bid to move its headquarters to New York City in February 2019, Democratic congresswoman Alexandria Ocasio-Cortez held a community town hall with her constituents.[7] "If Jeff Bezos wants to be a good person," she said, "he'd turn Amazon into a worker cooperative."[8] AOC's punchy call for a radical transformation of Amazon's everything store was driven by the company's long history of bad behavior.[9] Predictably, the e-commerce titan has been the target of 1.3 million workers' strikes, a steady stream of lawsuits, antitrust policy proposals, and calls for nationalization.[10]

Ocasio-Cortez was the first prominent figure to advocate for the radical transformation of Amazon into a worker cooperative. And since her remarks, there has been little in-depth exploration of what a cooperative Amazon might look like, or whether it is even feasible.

The suggestion of transforming de facto monopolies like Amazon into worker cooperatives is based on the belief that centralized-multistakeholder platforms, which are more probable as a model for marketplaces, have the potential to rival the dominance of the unstoppable "dark lord of online shopping" while providing a globally accessible service that is believed to be more ethical. While cooperative banks and extensive cooperative retail networks may exhibit only subtle distinctions from their competitors, they are often considered to be still a cut above mainstream businesses in terms of their ethical practices and community impact. Platform cooperatives, including AOC's envisioned cooperative Amazon, are often hailed as "anti-monopoly hammers" and democratic alternatives that confront the challenges presented by dominant platforms. According to Neal Gorenflo, co-founder and publisher of Shareable, platform co-ops offer a viable and ethical alternative to the formidable "Death Stars" of the digital economy.[11]

Stacco Troncoso, co-founder of DisCO and Guerilla Media Cooperative, shares this view. "We should outcompete the big players," he told me. "We can because we don't have to answer to shareholders as the first priority."[12] The Finnish cooperator Leo Sammallahti has echoed this in comments posted to the Platform

Co-op Discussion forum, writing, "we should have the ambition and confidence to seek a world where we replace the dominating capitalist actors."[13] I completely embrace the enthusiasm for creating something new and inspiring, fully committed to this journey. We shouldn't limit ourselves to what appears possible. However, we shouldn't solely focus on supplanting digital tycoons either. We can embrace the idea of building something beautiful and transformative that can coexist alongside them, too.

For now, although not inconceivable, even the mightiest platform cooperative would be an unlikely contender to outflank a multibillion-dollar tech company, and expecting a young grassroots movement to outcompete these tech empires would be akin to asking a five-year-old to hike for eleven hours while carrying a sixty-pound backpack.[14]

Platform cooperatives should be established and managed to *compete* with these corporate players—indeed, they have no choice but to do so—and aim to win significant secondary or tertiary roles in their markets. However, it can be difficult to compete with businesses that violate labor laws or engage in price dumping. But this is the approach of Eva and Drivers Cooperative, two cooperatives that vie with Lyft in Quebec and New York City. Stocksy United has carved out a space for itself against Getty Images. Up & Go competes with Handy and TaskRabbit.

According to research, cooperatives coexist with large corporations, but they have also been known to outpace them in certain instances, such as in Finland, Spain, and the Emilia-Romagna region of Italy. One study shows how Dutch community cooperative banks have successfully scaled to compete and coexist with heavily capitalized corporate banks.[15] The key contributing factor to the success of cooperatives over corporate rivals in these territories is the diligent effort of municipalities to enforce existing labor and environmental regulations, thereby ensuring that corporate competitors bear the full costs of their operations.

Aside from the challenges of implementation, it's not clear that a cooperative monopoly modeled after Amazon is even desirable. Cooperatives that have successfully "scaled up, out, and deep" have generally used an ecosystem approach to establish networks of smaller cooperatives, often beginning with a bank, credit union, or social security cooperative. This enables cooperatives—in the arts, health care, ride-hailing, and food delivery—to remain small, local, and responsive, while the alliance grows large enough to assist members in competing in regional and national markets. At the same time, the cooperatives can serve each other's members in a deepening web of support institutions.

At the local, national, and transnational levels, there exist a number of small cooperative commonwealths; some are nascent, others robust. Evergreen Cooperatives in Cleveland, Ohio, is made up of various businesses ranging from eco-friendly laundries and a solar energy company to urban farms, all of which are co-owned by more than 200 workers, many from low-income families.[16] In Mississippi, the Cooperation Jackson initiative includes a variety of enterprises, a federation of worker co-ops, a co-op incubator, a financial institution, as well as a sustainable housing project aimed at combating legacies of poverty and racial injustice. National and regional cooperative commonwealths in Finland, Italy, and India integrate worker and union co-ops from various sectors into mutually supportive networks.[17]

La Zona (The area), an experimental platform cooperative in Catalonia, is an intriguing example of a cooperative commonwealth that aspires to challenge the dominance of Amazon. It started with Opcions, the communication unit of a co-op for ethical consumption that partnered with several other cooperatives to provide a long-term, local, ethical alternative to large online retailers such as Amazon. La Zona's marketplace registered 100 businesses within a year of its launch in 2021, with seed grants from Catalonia's autonomous government and the city of Barcelona—clearly not enough to cause panic on Amazon's white-collar floors, but it's a beginning. According to the founders, La Zona places a premium on proximity between buyers and sellers. They have fifty hubs from which they deliver parcels by foot, bicycle, and scooter; couriers are paid a flat rate regardless of the number of parcels delivered.

Seeded with a modest initial funding of €160,000 from Catalonia's autonomous government and an additional €50,000 from the city of Barcelona, the example of La Zona marketplace highlights the need for these marketplaces to scale beyond a region and secure funding from a broad network of supporters, extending beyond reliance on state or municipal funding, within an eccosystem of small businesses and other allies. In an interview, Opcions spokesperson José Alonso said, "Do you know the saying 'Small is beautiful'? I believe we need to get past this thinking. Medium is nice, too. And we will see in ten years whether big is also beautiful. If we still exist."[18]

The spectrum of sizes invoked by Alonso raises a key point about cooperative scaling: different sectors will require different structures and sizes, appropriate to their missions and the communities they serve. Cooperative commonwealths can also coexist with other business models of varying size, such as publicly owned digital platforms, unionized venture-backed platforms, and hybrids. And all that with a firm eye on the commons.

Depending on the sector, platform co-ops can operate locally, globally, or somewhere in between. Diverse scaling strategies are demonstrated by the various local businesses associated with the Zona marketplace, by federations such as India's SEWA, and by the mutual-risk platform co-op Smart, which now operates in seven European countries. Scaling that bridges rich countries with the Global South can and must address structural inequities, as some global cooperative coffee networks have demonstrated.

~

One of the most exciting aspects of cooperatives right now is their ability to scale online without incurring the brick-and-mortar costs associated with traditional co-ops. Small producers can band together online to expand their reach, operating as a single entity or an affiliated group under a digital umbrella platform. "One of the most appealing things about platform cooperatives, in contrast to their offline cousins, is their ability to replicate and scale," writes the American economist and sociologist Juliet Schor.[19]

The idea of an internationalist federation of cooperative digital platforms is promising. By leveraging a new digital infrastructure of distributed ledgers, smart contracts, and data trusts, an emerging distributed internet, also known as Web3, is creating novel pathways for platforms to scale. These technologies will enable replication, social franchising, and conversion in previously unseen forms via shared digital infrastructure.

In 2016, business professor Jeremy Rifkin stirred up controversy at the annual conference of the International Cooperative Alliance in Quebec by contending that the digital revolution presented a once-in-a-lifetime opportunity to establish cooperatives of considerable scale—even on par with that of Amazon. "If such a [digital] cooperative model did not already exist, it would have to be created," he said.[20]

Then, as now, not everyone is convinced. That includes many who agree in principle that it's "better for people to own the monopolies than for the monopolies to own the people," as the 1898 Labor Annals put it.[21] According to British scholar Nick Srnicek, attempting to match "the vast resources of [dominant] companies" would require platform cooperatives to emulate "the monopolistic nature of platforms." Besides which, Srnicek argues, such scaling is almost certainly impossible in any case. "A platform like Facebook would still have the weight of its existing data, network effects, and financial resources to fight off any co-op rival."[22]

While much of this holds true, it is also important to refrain from grounding twenty-first-century criticisms of cooperative scaling in nineteenth-century arguments leveled against legacy cooperatives, namely consumer cooperatives. Specifically, they echo Rosa Luxemburg's pamphlet, *Reform or Revolution*, which conceded a limited, tactical benefit to consumer cooperatives— they could, she wrote, create "the germs of the future social order while developing the growing organization and class conscious-ness of the working class"—only to then dismiss them as "the economic points of support for the theory of revisionism [and] a return to the puny worn-out slippers of the bourgeoisie."[23] Today, it is crucial to understand that cooperatives are not homogeneous entities, with multi-stakeholder cooperatives deserving special attention as they extend beyond their membership and often have a profound influence on a larger community.

Traces of this argument are visible in the American sociologist Juliet Schor's book *After the Gig*. "The ambitions of community-based start-ups to solve the problems identified by the idealist discourse have mostly gone unfulfilled, especially in the United States," she writes. "None has scaled like the big platforms. Many have folded. Others are viable, but we find they are reproducing aspects of the conventional economy they were hoping to escape, including race, class, and gender exclusion."[24]

There is some truth here. The power of existing network-effect advantages should not be downplayed. Nor should the fact that most VC-funded start-ups also fail. And it's also worth remembering that throughout history, the majority of coopera-tives have emerged as a response to market failures, born out of necessity rather than some kind of killer instinct that drives them to destroy monopolies. It is true that, with a few exceptions, plat-form cooperatives have not reached the same scale as corporate platforms. Platform co-ops emerge, fail, or persevere alongside monopolies.

To this end, brick-and-mortar cooperatives stand to benefit from the scaling potential of the digital economy's "long tail," the strategy of generating high revenue at low volume—say, by sourcing niche or rare goods to large numbers of customers. The more co-ops cooperate under platforms, the easier it becomes to imagine something like a cooperative alternative to Amazon's everything store. It would not be a monopoly in any familiar sense of the word, but rather a multi-stakeholder platform of independent but federated co-ops supported by national and international networks of cooperative suppliers, managers, upstream supply-chain workers, logistics and tech workers, and customers. Something like La Zona, but replicated across the planet.

If too-broad dismissals of platform scaling are misplaced, so is naive optimism about it. Growth brings challenges in terms of member engagement, participation, and governance. The Uralungal Labor Contract Co-operative Society, India's oldest worker cooperative, with more than 1,415 members, is embroiled in scandals caused by opaque contracting. India's Amul Dairy, the world's largest dairy cooperative with more than 3 million members of small farms, is widely criticized for benefiting middle- to upper-income farmers at the expense of poor workers. But if the evidence is mixed on large co-ops outperforming their corporate counterparts in social justice metrics, there are also compelling models showing that better things are possible. Mondragon, a federation of 240 consumer and worker co-ops headquartered in the Basque Country, comprises eighty-three cooperatives with a total of 68,743 employees and is dedicated to supporting the Sustainable Development Goals of the United Nations while adhering to ten ethical guiding principles. Orona and Ulma, two major members of Mondragon's industrial division, left the co-op network late in 2022, shaking the federation's stability after sixty years in operation. The departure of these companies, which accounted for 15 percent of income and 13 percent of employment across the network, does not call Mondragon's existence or ideals into question, but it does invite other questions about how to best scale cooperative networks.

The arguments against the promise and potential of scaling are belied by the sheer volume and multiplicity of cooperative activity around the world, in particular in the United States, where one in every three people participates in one or more of the approximately 65,000 cooperative institutions, including housing co-ops.[25] American credit unions alone have more than 100 million members. Indeed, more US citizens belong to a co-op than participate in the stock market. For centuries, agricultural co-ops, in the United States and throughout the world, have served as risk-management engines, providing health benefits, lower prices, and community. While the specific benefits bestowed upon people may vary, cooperatives with a wide reach often operate as an underground current, generating substantial advantages and influencing economies and communities.

The United States is not an outlier among wealthy countries. Italy is home to a substantial number of worker cooperatives, totaling 29,414, with the majority of them founded since 1991. In Spain, there are 17,000 co-ops employing around 210,000 people, while in Finland, cooperative groups dominate the milk production sector, and 81 percent of the country's population are members of cooperatives. Additionally, Denmark's primary retailer operates proudly as a cooperative.[26]

According to a 2017 report by CICOPA—the International Cooperative Association's branch that represents worker, producer, and social co-ops—more than 27 million people worldwide work in cooperatives, 16 million as employees and more than 11 million as worker-members.[27] According to data from the 2014 United Nations Census, 250 million people worldwide are employed "in or within the scope of 2.5 million cooperatives."[28]

These studies reveal roughly equal amounts of cooperative activity in the Global South and high-income countries.[29] In India, the Kerala Dinesh Cooperative Society currently directly employs 6,000 people. In Kenya, cooperatives directly employ more than 300,000 people.

These figures, though impressive, are incomplete, as the World Cooperative Monitor is heavily reliant on self-reported data. However, the available data indicate that cooperatives are not nearly as economically marginal or isolated as they are frequently portrayed. The emphasis on market share obscures what is most important: the actual values, practices, and outcomes produced by cooperative enterprises, and the potential for amplifying their impact through federation and thoughtful scaling.

The Platform Cooperativism Consortium has cataloged roughly 543 digital platform projects in more than forty-nine countries, painting a picture of the emerging landscape that allows us to identify the most important success stories and their types. They include Smart, the 35,000-member mutual-risk platform cooperative. NeedsMap, a social platform co-op with a lower membership requirement, has more than a million members. Let's review some of the most promising of these in turn.

The platform co-op Smart, or Société Mutuelle Pour Artistes, is an imaginative illustration of scaling. [30] The co-op describes itself as "the missing link between the precariat and the salariat." Smart transforms independent contractors into co-op employees, providing them with legal protections while also paying freelancers promptly. "The most important thing for us is to find a way to adapt existing social protections to new work realities," one of its leaders told me.[31] In its home country of Belgium, Smart represents 34,219 members, including designers, painters, information technology consultants, virtual reality technicians, stage designers, and sculptors. In 2021, Smart billed more than €164 million in revenue.

Freelancers typically find their own gigs while navigating administrative mazes and fluctuating cash flows, which can make freelancing a strenuous quest. Smart employs freelancers on short-term contracts and negotiates the terms of their work directly with clients (price, timeline, scope).[32] By handling invoicing and payment collection, Smart alleviates one of the most common aggravations of freelance life: the fear of not being paid on time, or at all. Smart guarantees that the worker will be paid in full within seven working days of completing the assignment and even provides a "small business toolbox" for bookkeeping, invoicing, and insurance management. This provision, which relieves creative freelancers of administrative burdens, is at the heart of Smart's unofficial slogan: "Vous créez, nous gérons!" (You create, we manage!).[33]

Crucial to Smart's mission of pooling resources to create a commons, 2 percent of each invoice is allocated to the Mutual Guarantee Fund. In this regard, Smart performs a role akin to that of unions, providing support for its members. As Gar Alperovitz notes, "any serious future politics will have to find some other way—if it can!—to do what labor unions once did."[34] Smart is effectively following organizations of nonunion workers, such as the National Domestic Workers Alliance, which have been cropping up more frequently in the United States in recent years; both co-ops and these "alt-labor" organizations provide protections for informal work arrangements that previously did not exist in this form.

One day in 2016, I met the then managing director of Smart's Belgian branch in a hotel in Brussels. Sandrino Graceffa is a short, powerfully built man with dark, glistening eyes who began his career in the social economy at a young age. He grew up in a mining town in northern France as the son of a coal miner in a family of ten children. It was a company town, and the mine bosses micromanaged every aspect of workers' lives, from housing to community events and social life. Graceffa's early development of a strong Marxist vision was influenced by this family history. Rather than becoming directly involved in progressive party politics, he chose to experiment with entrepreneurial cultures defined by economic autonomy.

It was Graceffa's vision to turn Smart into a cooperative after Pierre Burnotte and Julek Jurowicz founded it as a new type of mutual aid society for creative gig-economy freelancers.[35] Launched as a not-for-profit organization, Smart became a cooperative in 2017.[36] Today, it operates independently in seven countries. While the digital platform is paramount to Smart's operation in Belgium, the affiliate in Spain, so far, makes no use of the digital platform. (This is just as well, as the software Smart uses in Belgium is based on that country's legal and tax structures, and not easily adapted for use in other countries.)

Along with successfully replicating its model across Europe, Smart has inspired a similar freelance cooperative in the US called Guilded, a cooperative committed to supporting artists and all creatives. For demonstrating how its model can be replicated across diverse work cultures and legal frameworks, Smart is increasingly recognized as a scaling pioneer. "We think that's really the game changer," says Guilded's Melissa Hoover.

The Smart example shows that there is no universally applicable one-size-fits-all blueprint or technical infrastructure for platform cooperatives. The independence of national nodes has been critical to the platform's scaling. The next major test will involve scaling the Smart model and its principles to the sizable informal sectors of the Global South. Although the formalization of work through digital platforms has the potential to provide greater economic security for India's informal sector workforce, it is important to recognize that it is not a straightforward or unambiguous solution. While more than 90 percent of India's workforce is engaged in the informal sector, it is uncertain whether the formalization of work through digital platforms will truly benefit these workers. It may compel workers to pay taxes and other regulatory fees, for instance, and also open them up to state and commercial surveillance.

While not legally considered a social franchise, Smart has served as a model for various platform cooperatives looking to replicate its approach in different countries. However, despite benefiting from the guidance and support provided by Smart BE, the cooperative that first established the Smart model in Belgium, some of Smart's European partners assert their independence from it.

The Montreal-based Eva Global, on the other hand, employs a different approach to scaling. Eva Global intentionally structured itself as a corporation rather than a cooperative in order to secure funding and ensure its survival. While this corporate structure may raise concerns for worker cooperatives, it serves as a strategic approach for the company to sustain itself and support worker co-ops worldwide. While Eva's social franchise model, which allows drivers to retain a larger portion of the revenue they generate, holds significant promise, the rules imposed by this model do not always align with the desires and capabilities of specific off-spring co-ops. Eva is partnering with local taxi cooperatives to implement its blockchain-based e-hailing technology solution, a model that requires these local co-ops to have some financial resources as a precondition for joining the franchise.

Similar to the franchise model is *replication*, in which a new business simply applies an existing template, usually including open-source or source-available software. One example that I discussed earlier is Up & Go, a platform co-op that serves as an umbrella for three local cooperatives sharing digital infrastructure. The local aspects of working with the co-op members on a daily basis have not changed; they have simply become more streamlined. Instead of stumbling upon new customers through leaflets pinned to local laundromat bulletin boards, new and often more affluent clientele access the service through the app. Up & Go plans to replicate the New York City model in Philadelphia and also abroad.

The physical proximity of co-op members living in a particular location facilitates decision-making. When scaling up through a platform, however, it is important to ensure that democratic governance is not compromised. Up & Go, for instance, maintains human connection within their cooperative network by allowing small worker co-ops to join under the umbrella of the platform, enabling them to scale while preserving human trust. When members are geographically dispersed, it is difficult to keep emotional ties to the co-op community. Stocksy United's members, for example, are spread across sixty-five countries. The platform co-op addresses this by providing a member dashboard on its website, essentially an automated resolution system, where members can express and discuss their concerns.

A similar innovation-minded approach to scaling defined the platform co-op Consegne Etiche in Bologna, Italy. The organization's origins date to the early months of the COVID-19 pandemic, when the Municipality of Bologna's Foundation for Urban Innovation conducted a series of interviews with residents to determine the best way to assist them during the crisis. The city conducted more than 150 interviews with community members from a variety of backgrounds, including shopkeepers, a cooperative consortium, food delivery couriers, student organizations, urban planners, various volunteer groups, and other local institutions.[37] Based on the findings, the city established a platform co-op for home deliveries in collaboration with local merchants, couriers, and Bologna residents.[38] Consegne Etiche, a response to the pandemic, was born.

Unlike courier jobs with corporate platforms such as Deliveroo, DoorDash, and UberEats, which typically pay between six and seven euros per hour, Consegne Etiche jobs pay nine euros per hour and include safety and labor protections such as accident and medical insurance. In total, the jobs provide an additional five euros per hour in wages and benefits.

Consegne Etiche is one of the first platform co-ops for home delivery that respects courier rights while also considering the environment—all deliveries are by bicycle. Although the establishment of Consegne Etiche—through the involvement of municipalities and manifestos that prioritize workers' rights and protections, including fair pay and safe working conditions—provides an exemplary model that cities worldwide can follow, the platform co-op's scaling potential was limited due to a lack of focus on the realities of running a business. Consegne Etiche consciously rejects reputation systems that could foster competition among workers. These are the systems that allow customers to score workers, which with VC-backed platforms can easily lead to the firing of workers. These platform principles were enshrined in the city of Bologna's "fundamental charter of digital workers."[39]

Headquartered in Paris, CoopCycle is a platform serving a federation of bicycle-delivery cooperatives, providing a digital bicycle logistics infrastructure that manages deliveries and provides services to restaurants, shops, and other clients through their "Coopyleft-licensed" open-source software, which consists of a web platform and a mobile app. Only worker cooperatives or collectives using bicycles are given the opportunity to join. More than sixty courier cooperatives, mostly in Western Europe, currently share the software and are members of the federation. It's a great example of scaling through federation, which is now also gaining traction in Argentina and beyond.

Can co-ops in sectors like manufacturing and culinary services scale their businesses effectively in the digital economy? A major test case of scaling is under way involving Mondragon. It's important to acknowledge that even with its co-op network model and steadfast commitment to sustainability, Mondragon, like any organization, has areas where it can continue to grow and evolve. Problematically, only 83 of the 240 companies in Mondragon's network are cooperatives, the majority of which are located in the Basque region, where approximately 30,300 worker-members enjoy shared ownership, participation in decision-making, and profit sharing. They make up 44.1 percent of Mondragon's total workforce, while the remaining 157 noncooperative subsidiaries are spread out, with 40.9 percent located elsewhere in Spain and 15 percent abroad. These facts raise justifiable questions about the feasibility of scaling up co-ops while retaining the benefits that they promised at launch, pointing to the tensions surrounding the compatibility of cooperative models with capitalist systems that have been subject to discussion since their inception. Reflecting the pressures of globalization and to benefit its Basque member-ship and scale solidarity, Mondragon has had to draw on supply chains from Poland to Brazil and China, a strategy that is not unlike that of capitalist companies. Mondragon is comprised, for example, of traditional cooperatives that manufacture electro-magnetic equipment, garden furniture, consoles, and gears for the world's leading automobile manufacturers. Each company that wants to join the network must adhere to the company's principles and cannot compete with an existing business within the network. Mondragon states that its wage ratios between executive work and minimum-wage field or factory work have been agreed upon in various cooperatives, ranging from 3:1 to 9:1, with a median of 5:1.[40] Compare that to the United States, where the CEOs of the largest 350 companies earn approximately 320 times as much as the typical worker.[41]

In the summer of 2019, when I first visited Mondragón, or Arrasate as it is known in Basque, I was guided by Ander Etxe-berria, a sociologist and engineer who has worked for Mondragon for over a decade. He started our tour of the city and its cooperatives at a monument to José María Arizmendiarrieta, a twenty-six-year-old Catholic priest inspired by economic distributism's social teachings who helped found the network of cooperatives in 1955. Mondragon grew as a result of the priest's determined scaling abilities. Following the Spanish Civil War, he spent a decade organizing debates about the economy and political system, as well as raising funds for the first co-op through bake sales and small donations. Arizmendiarrieta "talked about changing the world, but what he really meant was changing the region," Etxeberria explained.

While we waited in line at a cooperative gas station, I asked Etxeberria if he believed that Mondragon could be replicated in other countries. He raised his eyes to mine and categorically stated, "They can't even repeat it behind this mountain," pointing across the Deba River. "The company was founded in the immediate wake of World War II, when the population was starving and the society was more religious. You could start another company like this, but it would have to be different." Perhaps replicating the company elsewhere in the world would be as wrongheaded as attempting to create another Silicon Valley outside of California. There is, however, no consensus on this at Mondragon University. One professor contended that the cooperative network has never been replicated only because such a thing has never been seriously attempted.

Mondragon's geographical location in a culturally homogeneous region, where values such as cooperation, an all-defining affinity with Basque identity, and social responsibility are shared, aided in the creation of its network. It began with the appliance manufacturer Fagor Electrodomésticos, the credit union Caja Laboral, the social-security cooperative Lagun Aro, and the consumer-worker hybrid cooperative Eroski. Remarkably, this business network in the Mondragón Valley prospered and made a significant impact on the national economy, even in the absence of a railway system, as all products had to be transported by trucks on narrow roads out of the low-lying basin.

Connecting these contexts, an additional method of scaling involves the conversion of existing legacy cooperatives into platform cooperatives. Although this approach has not been explored at Mondragon thus far, it holds promise, particularly for the culinary foundation within the network. By leveraging the existing logistics of platforms and their user base, this model attempts to overcome the "cold-start problem," or the challenges of starting a digital platform business from scratch.

Conversion is the least battle-tested of the models of scaling around the world—at least in the digital realm. One form of conversion in the world of manufacturing is recuperation, which was used in the case of more than 200 traditional companies in Argentina between 2001 and 2002 in the aftermath of the country's financial crisis, when workers took over failing factories and turned them into cooperatives. Today, there are 16,000 workers in about 400 recuperated, or converted, factories in Argentina.[42] But surely these are not digital businesses. How might conversion apply to the scaling of digital platforms? This is an emerging field of experimentation, but clearly it would involve finding ways to allow start-ups already incorporated as for-profit entities to transition to entities defined by community and worker ownership. To this end, Nathan Schneider has proposed that a company can transition to a structure where it's owned not just by investors or the original founders, but by employees and its own customers by way of a "trust buyout," where the users and workers buy out the investors.[43] A "user trust" allows the start-up's employees to take out loans to buy company shares on behalf of the members of the cooperative. Such "exit to community" is a viable method for conversion to platform cooperatives and adjacent models.

A more common method of scaling, beyond conversion, is the federation model, where multiple smaller cooperatives collectively own and manage a shared digital platform. This forms a second-level cooperative known as a platform co-op, allowing them to connect with clients and expand their reach. Cooperatives have a long history of forming alliances that span large geographic areas. India's SEWA Federation and the Basque Country's Mondragon are two examples. According to one co-op scholar, a federating strategy allows "cooperatives [to] form relations up and down-stream in the production process with other cooperatives, creating an interlocking group of consumer and producer cooperatives."[44]

SEWA exemplifies how a federation can force-multiply the power of individual cooperatives. Take the story of how the federated co-ops addressed their financial powerlessness not long after the organization's founding. In the early 1970s, banks in Gujarat refused to give women in the informal sector access to credit, claiming they were too risky and ultimately "not bankable." In 1972 and 1973, SEWA founder Ela Bhatt organized a series of meetings with women who were forced to take out loans from moneylenders at high rates of interest that left them debt-ridden. On the banks of the Sabarmati River, the women of SEWA hammered out an alternative solution.

It was a wrinkled vendor named Chandaben who first suggested, "Why don't we open our own bank?" When another SEWA member responded that they were "too poor" to succeed, the old vendor responded with the words that have since become central to organizational lore: "Yes, we are poor. But we are many!" Four thousand women raised the seed capital, and within a year, the first women-owned and -managed bank in India, the SEWA Cooperative Bank, was registered in the state of Gujarat.

Members learned to sign their own names, and then set up their own bank. They formed a social security co-op, and soon thereafter a pharmacy and an Ayurvedic production co-op. The co-ops in this federated "ecosystem" aimed "to organize women workers into cooperatives for full employment and self-reliance."[45]

SEWA's integrative, federal model of meeting social and economic needs on a national scale has been key to empowering poor self-employed women in India's vast informal economy. This is not a static model, but a work in progress, with new forms and members appearing on a regular basis. SEWA is currently experimenting with the formation of platform cooperatives owned and led by women, such as, in farming, Megha Adivasi Mahila Agricultural Producers' Cooperative. But SEWA is also keen to develop a collaborative online marketplace for a wide range of their artisanal products, such as snacks, garments, generic pharmaceuticals, and Ayurvedic medicines.[46]

As platform scaling matures, it is likely to be impacted by the rise of decentralized autonomous organizations, or DAOs, one of the more futuristic aspects of blockchain. A DAO is a new type of organizational structure in which the instrument for co-ownership is the blockchain. A blockchain is a digital, decentralized ledger of transactions that is secure and immutable due to its cryptographic links between blocks of data. Each block contains a timestamp, a hash of the previous block's unique identifier, and transaction data, creating a chain of blocks that is resistant to tampering or revision. By leveraging this structure, many technologists have established "crypto co-ops," but the term is often improperly used due to a lack of familiarity with the defining principles of cooperative identity.

Because it was supposed to be a decentralized Kickstarter, the first DAO is a good example of the co-op ethos. In general, the creation of DAOs does not always culminate in a conversion. DAO-ification, in which organizations decentralize ownership by tokenizing their shares, is a clearer illustration of conversion.

Each of these conversion models can help hierarchical organizations decentralize decision-making and ownership. In the words of the organizations Lensational, Krak, and the soon-to-be platform cooperative Hylo, they provide maps for organizations seeking an "exit to community."

Scaling models will always benefit from the support provided by "anchor institutions," a term chiefly developed by Karen Fulbright-Anderson, Patricia Auspos, and Andrea Anderson.[47] In Preston, Northern England, the Labour-led city council incubated an ecosystem of ten worker cooperatives while channeling all procurements exclusively to local businesses. The list continues: the Center for Family Life in New York, which provides support staff, training, and funding leads; Incubator.coop in Australia, which collaborates with the national co-op association BCCM to service innovative cooperatives; and the Sunset Park Family Center supported Up & Go. Mobicoop, a transportation-booking platform in France, would not exist without its close ties to municipalities, which supported its provision of last-mile services, which combined taxi services, particularly in rural areas, with trains.[48] (To this list of "midwives of the movement," I would humbly add my own organization, the Platform Cooperativism Consortium.)

Anchor organizations provide vital logistical support to platform co-op pioneers—and many co-ops would not have gotten off the ground without assistance during incubation—and ensure continuity during changes in local government.

Francesca Bria's work as Barcelona's chief technology officer revealed the need for more emphasis on financing and developing extra-governmental institutions capable of carrying on her critical agenda when the local government changes.

Finally, anchor institutions contribute to a movement's long-term viability by serving as a constant point of contact to ensure that values are consistently promoted, resources are brought to bear on the work, and organization and coordination are carried out in a systematic and inclusive manner. Local governments, municipalities, can play important anchoring roles in progressive states in otherwise capitalist societies by providing conducive regulation, if not direct, continuous support for cooperatives.

The cooperative's ability to scale continues to be greatly influenced by its close relationship with the government. Indeed, this holds true in the southern Indian state of Kerala, where the state government has faced accusations of favoring the construction cooperative Uralungal Labour Contract Co-operative Society (ULCCS) at the expense of transparency and democratic processes in the allocation of government contracts.[49] While states and national governments can assist cooperatives in their expansion, it is for this reason that co-ops should assert their independence after the start-up phase. Continued reliance on government funding carries obvious risks; cooperatives should be bottom-up institutions, not top-down ones.

I had the honor of addressing these and other issues in a talk delivered before Kerala's Legislative Assembly in Thiruvananthapuram in the fall of 2019. In the expansive setting of the Niyamasabha Complex, I had the opportunity to speak, capturing the government's keen interest in ways to enhance the integration of platform co-ops in Kerala.

The man who introduced me, Thomas Isaac, the state's finance minister and a major benefactor of the ULCCS, reviewed and countered many of the widely shared objections to the worker co-op model sketched above. He argued that starting new cooperatives is difficult and capital-intensive, and that states like Kerala can help by providing capital and support. This was all too rare, he said, because mainstream economists still believe cooperatives are inherently inefficient. In my remarks, I added that in the absence of strong state support, federated digital platforms can help aggregate services and products for under-resourced federated cooperatives.

Following my presentation, I spoke with P. K. Jayashree, the registrar of Cooperative Societies in Kerala, who asked me in a room full of lawyers how the government could help launch platform cooperatives in the south of India through regulation. How should they change the law? What was needed? Platform co-ops, I responded, should receive start-up funding but not be tethered to or run by the state. I replied that in a partner state, cooperatives certainly benefit from start-up funding from government and other sources, but ultimately, they should be voluntary and autonomous organizations.

Beyond that, I explained, the primary role of government should be to provide conducive regulation. In the United States, the history of very large cooperatives—credit unions, agricultural co-ops, and rural electric cooperatives—demonstrates that scaling is inextricably linked to regulation. As a matter of government policy, President Franklin D. Roosevelt made all three types of co-ops possible during the New Deal. With Executive Order No. 7037 in 1935, he established the Rural Electrification Administration, and two years later, he passed the Electric Cooperative Corporation Act, which authorized the formation and operation of consumer-owned electric cooperatives. Because regulation is critical to cooperative success, legal scholars must team up with cooperative practitioners to develop policy proposals, teach about cooperatives in law schools, and value cooperatives as a means to counter platform capitalism.

Still, there are no guarantees. Poorly thought-out co-op regulation backfired in one well-known case in Brazil in the 1990s, when rapacious entrepreneurs established a slew of bogus cooperatives simply because cooperatives were only permitted to classify their workers as independent contractors, rather than employees, allowing these entrepreneurs to avoid paying workers the benefits and other guaranteed protections to which employees are legally entitled.

Also, today, there is cause for concern that some platform co-ops permit their members to be self-employed, without giving them employee-like benefits and protections.

Cooperatives that choose to scale, mercifully, are not obliged to do so. They don't have to become "worker-run behemoths" in order to help people who aren't protected by governments, markets, or communities—freelancers and others—by providing instruments that increase their power and reach.

As we have seen with Stocksy United, Smart, and others, maintaining democratic governance may be a challenge when scaling platform cooperatives, but it is not an insurmountable one. Here, additional research is needed into the future of distributed governance and the methodologies and technologies that will enable it.

While some cooperatives may choose to maintain a localized focus deeply rooted in their communities, others may opt for international expansion, attracting members from diverse parts of the world. A well-considered scaling strategy should embrace this diversity and avoid the false insistence that either small or big is inherently desirable. It is key to recognize that different industries mandate specific structures designed to meet their unique needs. Over the past five years, it is not only numerous small, locally based digital cooperatives that have achieved remarkable success, but also those that have successfully scaled up, particularly by embracing a federated approach. Based on the evidence from existing co-op networks that hold a quasi-monopoly status, the desirability or feasibility of a globally operated, dominant, and centralized cooperative platform, resembling Amazon but operating as a co-op, remains unclear. However, this does not imply that our imagination should be limited; instead, it should serve as a catalyst to envision a comprehensive system that fully embraces and scales cooperative values, encompassing everything "from A to Z."

4

Redefining Value

I met Tyler Cowen, an American economics professor and *New York Times* columnist, at a business conference held at Madrid's opulent Ritz Hotel in the fall of 2017. As I listened to his presentation on the event's theme, "The Second Machine Age: Organizing for Economic Prosperity," I recalled his book *Average Is Over*, in which he predicts that the emergence of a "superclass" will restructure the economy.

In the brave new world of this superclass, he wrote, "Making high earners feel better in just about every part of their lives will be a major source of job growth in the future."[1] As for the rest of us, Cowen surmised that non-superclass workers might earn between $5,000 and $10,000 annually. To get a sense of what this society might look like, he recommends contemporary Mexico as an inspiring example. After all, in Mexico "lodging [for the poor] is satisfactory, if not spectacular, and of course the warmer weather helps."[2]

I approached him between conference sessions with a question: Had he considered co-ops as an economic model that would allow us to aspire to something more than the "winner-takes-all" economy of the superclass?

Gazing at the ground, Cowen responded as if I had simultaneously embarrassed him and wasted his time with the question.

"Cooperatives make up an insignificant part of the gross domestic product," he said. "They are too marginal to consider."

With that, the *Times* columnist excused himself and turned around to avoid further discursive displeasure.

Had he shown any willingness to engage on the subject, I would have noted that, although cooperatives represent only 3 percent to 5 percent of the world's GDP, that number surges in many regions and countries around the world.[3] The annual reports of the Global Cooperative Monitor are a valuable resource for this topic. In Kenya, for instance, 43 percent of the GDP is generated by cooperatives.[4] In New Zealand, co-ops represent 18 percent of the GDP. The Netherlands and France also have a significant share of 18 percent. Finland follows closely with 14 percent. Meanwhile, in Emilia-Romagna, Italy, the formal cooperative economy accounts for a substantial 40 percent of the region's gross domestic product.[5]

The biggest problem with Cowen's dismissal is that it fails to appreciate that GDP is a highly contentious metric to begin with, one with a strong normative bias that is increasingly and hotly debated at the highest levels of policy making around the world. But even within its own logic, the GDP is an inadequate measure. It doesn't capture intangible factors that are important for the growth of productivity, such as innovations that impact capital investment. Regarding the value system embedded in the GDP index, the American politician Robert F. Kennedy was ahead of this reevaluation when he noted in 1967 in Detroit, "The gross national product measures everything except that which makes life worthwhile."[6]

Worker cooperatives are defined by their own terms—not those of Cowen or other mainstream "growth" economists. They are not designed or geared to create economic output for its own sake, but to generate social value for communities. The GDP is striking for its inability to measure such value.

When describing economic activity, quantitative indicators like GDP rarely reference their underpinning values at all—such values are considered "external" to the framework. But this view is increasingly under attack from scholars such as the American economist Sanjay Reddy, who argue that economic indicators are meaningless unless we clarify the values that drive them.[7] The GDP measures the "market value" of national output but is mute on the quality of life enjoyed by the people responsible for that output.

A 2013 study conducted by German researchers Christian Kroll and Sebastian Pokutta shows that what is most important to people is not quantifiable by GDP. The researchers asked their subjects to describe their idea of a "perfect day." They discovered that the majority of the test subjects' time was spent on relationships and social leisure activities such as eating. "To maximize well-being, it is likely that working and consuming (which increase GDP) will play a smaller role in people's daily activities in the future than it does now," the study's authors concluded.[8]

The idea that GDP—the sum of all "economic activity"—has limits is not new. Even the classical economist Adam Smith associated the wealth of nations with a sense of the public good related to the needs, desires, and conveniences of actual human beings.[9] GDP doesn't include the work of nonprofits, or account for the negative effects of economic activities such as environmental degradation.[10] GDP does not account for—indeed, it actively hides—work that is unpaid, such as domestic work, emotional care work, and reproductive labor.[11] The economist Mariana Mazzucato has claimed that the GDP undervalues the importance of government investment and incorrectly labels the banking sector "productive" when it is in fact "extractive." These limitations are compounded by the fact that GDP fails to capture intangible factors such as innovations that contribute to productivity growth; all that to say that the GDP is indeed a poor measure of economic activity and growth. Lastly, the infatuation with GDP highlights the absurdity of assuming the Western consumer lifestyle as the gold standard for a range of essentially incomparable countries and national cultures, thereby making it difficult to compare life- styles in different parts of the world.[12]

Cowen unapologetically upholds the "tyranny of the quanti- fiable," a way of thinking that, when taken to its logical conclusion, leads people to believe that social impacts, including those of cooperatives and other social enterprises, have a measurable "gene" that can be entered into spreadsheets just like data per- taining to finances.[13] But despite the growing presence of co-ops in the social economy, Cowen and his colleagues are uninterested in investigating their core elements and relative benefits. If they were more engaged, they'd soon discover the notion at the center of this chapter: value in the social economy.

One widely known counterpart of the GDP is Bhutan's Gross National Happiness index (GNH), introduced by the nation's prime minister in 1998 as a broad-based alternative to the GDP. International institutions such as the UN and several governments have since discussed the GNH as a new paradigm of development. For its implementation, Bhutan carries out a survey every five years, employing broad themes like psychological well-being, health, time use, education, culture, good governance, community vitality, ecology, and living standards. The Bhutanese government directly asks its own citizens about their spirituality, prayer and meditation habits, hours of sleep, and community involvement in a 300-question survey.

The GNH helped inspire the Organization for Economic Coop- eration and Development's "Better Life Index," created in 2011 to address the limits and failures of GDP as a guiding metric. The OECD metric, known as Gross National Well-being (GNW), ranks countries on numerous dimensions of well-being, including their quality of life, work, health, level of political participation, and overall "satisfaction." The OECD is currently working to incorporate measures of inequality in the GNW.

The Sustainable Development Goals (SDGs) adopted by the United Nations in 2015 reflect similar thinking. The plan encompasses seventeen sustainable development goals to be met by 2030. Spanning a wide range, the goals are nothing if not ambitious, and formalize a global commitment to end poverty and hunger, ensure good health and well-being, provide quality education and gender equality, and reinvent cities as places full of sustainable and climate-friendly innovation, responsible consumption, clean water, and strong institutions committed to justice.

The UN goals also serve as a North Star for cooperative federations such as the Mondragon network of consumer and worker co-ops. The UN Index's goal is to highlight the systemic changes required to address all people's basic needs. It tracks countries' progress in eradicating poverty, hunger, and AIDS and promoting gender equality.[14] The initiative presents a useful starting point for understanding the cooperative economy, because its philosophy and metrics share social DNA with countless co-ops worldwide. The goals provide a road map for developing alternatives to Tyler Cowen's GDP fixation, as well as a counterargument to those who use traditional metrics to maintain a highly unequal status quo.

Venezuela has a "Ministry of Supreme Social Happiness" that coordinates the government's social welfare programs with the goal of eliminating poverty. Ecuador and Bolivia have a different approach called "Buen Vivir" ("good living" or "living well" in Spanish) that incorporates Indigenous outlooks and emphasizes harmony with nature over economic development.

These alternative value systems propose that a country's collective well-being is not simply the result of a capitalist economy fixated on growth and concentrated wealth among elites. Instead, they offer alternative frameworks for understanding and promoting well-being. But how can cooperatives, particularly platform co-ops, create value and contribute to the advancement of the Sustainable Development Goals?

Bread and Roses for All

Meet.coop is a small-scale meeting and video-conferencing platform that uses BigBlueButton open-source software. Its members recognize that the multi-stakeholder co-op is unlikely to make a significant contribution to GDP or other national metrics. But they also understand that this isn't the point. A Meet.coop member pointed out on the Platform Cooperativism Discussion Forum that the goal is "not merely to scale and outcompete. We want to make interactions more meaningful in world-transforming ways. But, yeah, we can beat Zoom if we want to."[15]

If platform co-ops cannot compete with large corporations in revenue, what value do they add? That at least is the question many scholars pose, pointing to the "tyranny of the margin." The claim that cooperatives contribute "something else" begs the question of what that is. In the case of meet.coop, the claim that interactions are more meaningful than non-co-op alternatives suggests that a "genuine community" focus on democratic governance, data privacy, and a commitment to open source may be the answer.

Platform co-ops solve specific problems while pursuing a human-centric type of value. They are like an IKEA wrench, designed to fit specific screws and bolts, rather than a multipurpose tool like a Swiss Army knife.[16]

One of the key value propositions of numerous platform cooperatives, especially labor platforms, is material: they simply pay their members better than the market average or their venture-backed cousins. As American scholar Jessica Gordon-Nembhard, speaking about worker co-ops, summarizes it, "[Co-ops] place more emphasis on job security for employee-members and employees' family members, pay competitive wages (or slightly better than their sector), provide additional variable income through profit-sharing, dividends, or bonuses, and offer better fringe benefits."[17]

Along with contributing to the Sustainable Development Goals—especially those related to poverty, hunger, good health and well-being, and decent work—platform cooperatives also increase the value of labor and human capital. Whereas traditional businesses pay workers for their labor without offering ownership stakes in return, cooperatives typically provide workers not only ownership but also opportunities for training and development.

Another approach to thinking about the value created by co-ops is the "social good framework," a set of principles and practices that aim to enhance collective well-being and make the world more just and sustainable. In order to foster sustainable development, this strategy stresses participation while tackling social and environmental challenges. As American economist Robynn J. A. Cox explains:

> One of the most powerful implications of a theory of social good is its potential to insert into conversations on well-being, which typically focus on economic indicators, the resources needed for the efficient production of social goods and services . . . Society is typically interested in improving human capital because it improves productivity and, as a result, well-being. However, a social-good framework might also force society to not only think about the investments necessary to improve production of economic goods but to also consider the attributes, skills, and investments necessary to produce social goods more efficiently.[18]

A theory of social good can expand the discussion of well-being by articulating the resources required for the efficient production of social goods and services, instead of merely focusing on economic indicators. A number of reports and studies from the trenches of the cooperative economy back up this assessment. Consider Stocksy United, the stock photo and media platform co-op. In stark contrast to traditional photo services like Getty Images, the co-op offers a 50 percent to 75 percent split with photographers, the best share of profits in the stock photography industry. In home care, the Equal Care Cooperative in the UK has achieved similar success for its members. "I'm charging fourteen pounds an hour at the moment [and] contributing five percent to the office," said Daniel Cahill, one of Equal Care's members, when I interviewed him in 2021. "So, I'm making almost twice as much in the co-op."[19]

In ride hailing, the Canadian multi-stakeholder co-op Eva pays its drivers 10 percent more than Uber or Lyft. In the same industry, Drivers Cooperative, based in New York City, offers a competitive base rate of $30 per hour for all drivers—whether they have passengers or not. In the home-cleaning sector, the worker-owners that make up the American Up & Go cooperative earn an average of $25 an hour, compared with $18.03 an hour on average in the New York City metro area in 2019.[20] Unlike Handy, which keeps about 20 percent of the revenue, or Task-Rabbit, which keeps up to 30 percent, Up & Go keeps only 5 percent of workers' revenue to pay for platform operations and maintenance.[21] Out of that 5 percent, 3 percent goes to transaction processing for credit card companies and 2 percent to the maintenance of the platform itself—the stuff under the hood. Here again, we can note the overlap with UN SDGs concerned with poverty, hunger, health, and well-being.

It is not the case, however, that all members of platform cooperatives always receive equal shares of their co-op's income. I was standing on the stage at the 2017 platform co-op conference in New York, about to welcome the audience, when a friend approached me and whispered in my ear that she had learned that Stocksy

United does not share profits equally. She was visibly troubled by this, but I found her reaction somewhat unfair, considering that the inputs from producers themselves were also uneven. The platform pays twice the rate of Getty Images, after all. When a thousand people post their photos (a single shot or entire series of images) to the platform, it would not make sense for everyone to be paid the same, whether their images were purchased or not, and regardless of how often.

Equal wealth distribution is just not a proposal I associate with producer cooperatives that are owned and run by a community of artists, like Stocksy. For some of the artists, Stocksy United is their primary source of income, and they put enormous resources and energy into a single photo shoot. ("The high contributors invest [up] to $20,000 in some cases," notes American scholar Juliet Schor in her book *After the Gig*.) For others, it is merely a pastime. Hector, a photographer on the platform who uses it sparingly, described the occasional sale of his work as paying for "my beer, my bourbon, occasionally my dark rum, sometimes my light rum."[22]

It's worth noting that even within platform co-ops like Up & Go that offer equal hourly pay for all members, some members can choose to work more hours and thus earn more money. While not all platform cooperatives are based on perfect equality, platform worker cooperatives are vehicles of solidarity, aligning them with the UN development goal of providing "decent work" for all.

The benefits that contingent workers receive from a platform cooperative go far beyond higher wages. A key competitive advantage of platform co-ops is member ownership of software and their own intellectual property. This extends to a broad range of advantages and benefits related to transparency and privacy.

This can be seen in the way platform ownership allows communities to make the workings of the algorithm transparent to its users. The community can decide how to safeguard the privacy of users and workers to a greater degree than conventional, venture-backed platforms that have a mandate to extract and monetize user data. Due to the opaque nature of data flows—particularly those of upstream cloud services provided by large tech companies—it might be challenging for platform co-op founders to deliver data ownership as a set of rights pertaining to such data. For these founders, rather than attempting to lay claim to owning data, it's more meaningful to focus on controlling access and capture of data. Control and access transcend code, encompassing financial resources and budgets. Several platform co-ops such as Fairmondo and Ampled use transparent participatory budgeting tools, such as Open Budget.[23] This tool allows people to see how their organization spends money, for example. By tracking and presenting financial data in an easily comprehensible format, Open Budget software empowers citizens to hold their government (or their local platform co-op) accountable.

MIDATA, a platform co-op, holds a comprehensive collection of health data that patients are more likely to entrust to a cooperative than corporate entities, as it allows them to control how their data is shared. When a community of equals controls the software, abuses are far less likely. And it does not hurt that MIDATA is fortified with Swiss banking software. "In contrast to most of the current banking software where administrators have access to customer data, however, in [this] personal data platform each record is encrypted and only the account holder has the key."[24]

Of course, smaller platform co-ops have limited privacy protection as server maintenance can be expensive, leading to the popularity of cloud services like Amazon Web Services. While privacy tools in the crypto industry can offer anonymity, maintaining a public blockchain network can also be costly and unfeasible for some projects.

The social value created by co-ops extends beyond the relative control of software to the minutiae of workplace life. According to one global study, 85 percent of adults "are not engaged or [are] actively disengaged" at work.[25] Worker cooperatives, on the other hand, place a premium on engagement and participation. Research shows that worker cooperatives outperform traditional businesses in terms of productivity due to the higher levels of trust, involvement, knowledge sharing, and teamwork among co-op members.[26]

While glamorized, investor-owned gig platforms treat workers as replaceable labor, many platform co-ops invest in the education of their workers. The result? Workers in cooperatives skip fewer workdays and stay with the company longer. Stocksy United has even limited the number of its members to some 1,800 over ninety countries, in order to focus on developing the current workforce. Studies have also substantiated that after the start-up phase, worker co-ops are more resilient than traditional businesses in the face of the economic crises that beset capitalism. Comparative analyses of all businesses in countries such as Uruguay, Spain, and France shows that the survival rate of worker cooperatives is 16 percent greater compared with businesses in general.[27] Figures from the UK show that "co-operative startups [are] almost twice as likely to survive their first five years," compared with traditional companies.[28] Because worker co-ops are human-centered organizations that don't fold when they struggle with profitability, they are more resilient.

They are also more diverse. Approximately 50 percent of worker co-op members are women, and around 25 percent are Latino, according to the Democracy at Work Institute's 2022 survey of 180 worker cooperatives in the United States. In developing countries especially, large numbers of women join worker cooperatives. In India, this is seen in a 20,000-member strong sex worker co-op in the eastern city of Kolkata. Cooperatives can reverse the institutional exclusion faced by long-marginalized groups and create systems in which every member can flourish and be well regarded and treated as socially valuable.

Obran, a worker-owned cooperative conglomerate in Baltimore, has a portfolio of five companies encompassing tech staffing, construction, and outdoor furniture rentals. While their services are not targeted exclusively toward Blacks, Indigenous peoples, or other people of color, they strongly emphasize their commitment to being "pro-Black and pro-Brown" in line with their core values. Core Staffing, a platform cooperative, helps formerly incarcerated people find decent jobs. Computer scientist and Core Staffing co-founder Joseph Cureton explained: "When we launched in 2016, the project was initiated and led by returning citizens . . . the people who were doing the work. The project came out of the Bmore Black Techies Meetup."[29]

Feminist Approaches to Design

What might an intersectional feminist approach to designing platform co-ops look like? Chenai Chair, Mozilla's special advisor for Africa Innovation Mradi, proposes a feminist approach to digital platforms that addresses issues of access, skills, affordability, and "dataveillance," calling for a reconsideration of data collection and storage to avoid discrimination in South Africa based on factors such as race, ethnicity, location, health status, and gender.

Feminist and antiracist researchers in science and technology studies have highlighted that interlocking forms of oppression, such as sexism, white supremacy, and ableism, are integrated into the design of platforms and systems. This is more than just a matter of bias; it is a result of the ways that these forms of oppression are embedded in the very fabric of our technologies.[30] And as communities have control over platforms, they can better fight those biases.

Chair advocates for a feminist approach to building digital platforms that addresses discrimination against women of color, their safety, and the use of "shadow banning" to block feminist conversations.[31] An intersectional feminist approach to platform co-ops goes beyond inclusive hiring and encompasses a broader awareness of how data practices on the internet can impact people. Shadow banning is a practice in which a user's content is intentionally hidden from a wider audience without their knowledge or notification. "The very people who are developing search algorithms and architecture are willing to promote sexist and racist attitudes openly at work and beyond, while we are supposed to believe that these same employees are developing 'neutral' or 'objective' decision-making tools," notes the American internet studies scholar Safiya Umoja Noble.[32]

Chair defines a feminist approach to digital platforms as resistance through building social movements, shaping online public spaces, and developing new internet policies to humanize digital platforms and better serve workers and the community through participatory practices such as co-design, collective decision-making, and open-source software. Not incidentally, they also advance the Sustainable Development Goals that the UN has determined are urgently needed to achieve a fair, equitable, and sustainable world economy.

Platform cooperatives demonstrate their dedication to mitigating the escalating climate catastrophe by prioritizing environmental goals over profit maximization, emphasizing a commitment that extends beyond mere financial considerations. Katuma in Barcelona, for example, is a farm-to-table platform co-op that aims to create more eco-friendly food systems by improving solidarity in the food supply chain and promoting sustainable agricultural techniques. The platform includes individuals, consumer groups, and local producers who collectively own and manage the organization, and they also explore how new technologies can help farmers monitor climate data and transition to decentralized energy infrastructure.

Several large food delivery and courier platforms, meanwhile, have committed to zero-CO_2 emissions. These include CoopCycle and Consegne Etiche in Europe, which aspire to—and in most cases maintain—a bicycles-only policy. The latter platform touts this zero-emissions policy as a competitive advantage.

I already introduced La Zona, an ethical alternative to Amazon launched in Catalonia, Spain, earlier in this book. In 2021, the co-op united up to 1,000 cooperative businesses for shared order processing and delivery across seventeen Spanish provinces through fifty distribution hubs. To reduce CO_2 emissions, deliveries are made on foot, bicycles, and scooters. Participation in La Zona requires adherence to sustainability and governance standards, aligning with the SDG goal to build sustainable cities and communities.

In São Paulo, Brazil, a digital platform called Cataki allows recyclers and waste pickers (known locally as *catadores*) to learn where companies, building complexes, and the municipality dump recyclables such as scrap metal, bottles, and cartons. While not a cooperative, Cataki adheres to cooperative values. Launched in 2017 by a local artist who goes by the name of Mundano, Cataki connects residents and businesses to nearby catadores, who in aggregate are responsible for most recycling across Brazil, a country where less than 20 percent of the population has access to public recycling programs.

The Cataki platform is basic but effective: catadores use the Cataki app, and WhatsApp voice messages for those who can't read, to connect to their nearest waste collectors. As of this writing, more than 4,500 catadores have created accounts on Cataki; collectively, they manage in excess of 1,000 collections per month across the city. "All over the planet, there are 64 million 'invisible superheroes' like [these catadores] who are trying to save the planet, making an honest living from what people consider trash," says Mundano.

Because Brazil does not have a state-funded recycling program for household waste, the platform has not only created a new and safer employment sector for poor recyclers, it has also created a great deal of value to the public. The ecological impact of this work is crucial. By some estimates, up to 90 percent of all recycling that occurs in Brazil can be traced back to the work of roughly 400,000 catadores, who work mostly without union or co-op support. Although Cataki aggregates many of the waste pickers, it has yet to organize them.[33]

Similar informal recycling also takes place in Colombia and Egypt. The World Bank estimates that 1 percent of all city dwellers in the Global South currently work as waste-pickers. The recycling of paper, plastic, glass, and aluminum, it should be noted, is one of the SDGs established by the UN, which emphasizes that by 2050, the equivalent of almost three planets will be required to sustain our current lifestyles at current consumption rates. Here, again, there is an echo of the UN's development agenda in the work of Cataki and other catadores.

The world's crises stem from an excessive focus on economic growth, whereas cooperative businesses prioritize cooperation and empathy to address these issues. But in Indonesia, government-subsidized tech giants like Ruang Guru, Tokopedia, and Gojek monopolize access to resources, driven by venture capital and relentless growth. During my virtual meeting with cooperative maker Heida Hardiyanti, which was occasionally interrupted by her children, she explained that these venture capital–funded apps dominate the market in Indonesia. Their sole purpose? Growth at all costs.

"These VC-funded apps are the only way for people to get government resources," she explained. "People remain poor,

while these CEOs become increasingly wealthy. It's sickening."[34]
And while Indonesia has some 39 million cooperative members,
the government still does not legally recognize worker co-ops.
One of the earliest proto–platform co-ops in Indonesia was Beceer,
which began operating in East Java. The farm-to-table app was
critical during the pandemic.

At the Aqsa Farms in Java, I spoke with a group of urban quail
and maggot farmers who experiment with the platform co-op model
to keep young people involved in the agricultural sector. The res-
olute call of a cockerel frequently interrupted our conversation.
The children of farmers do not necessarily share their parents'
excitement about cooperatives (or farming). While new generations may perceive co-ops simply as the way older people do
business, experimenting with new technologies can contribute to
retaining young people in farming. During my presentation to an
Indonesian ministry, I learned that the Indonesian government is
currently promoting "digital cooperatives," with a reported count
of 250 in the country, which aligns with the fact that Indonesia's
population is comprised of 28 percent young people aged ten to
twenty-four, totaling 65 million individuals.[35]

Young people can play a crucial role in the success of cooperatives by taking part in decision-making, participating in overall
operations, and contributing fresh ideas, energy, and passion. A
recent study by the ICA Institute found that when young people
are involved in cooperatives, they are more likely to become life-
long members and active supporters of their local co-op.[36]

This was a common refrain also at a platform co-op conference
in Hong Kong in 2018, where representatives from a Taiwanese
eco-village sought to use technology to keep young people from
migrating to cities.[37] Henri Kasyfi discussed a cooperative platform for payment using facial recognition technology to help
street merchants, and Gigi Lo presented Translate for Her, a project that assists ethnic minority women in Hong Kong who cannot

read Chinese. Renowned sociologist Pun Ngai, co-author of *Dying for Apple: Foxconn and Chinese Workers*, argued that the challenge for platform cooperativism in Hong Kong is to not become an empty slogan but instead "a social movement embedded in real struggles." With 60 percent of the world's population residing in Asia, the cooperative digital economy holds immense potential to address urgent social and political challenges in the region, making a substantial impact on the lives of young people.

Cultures of Care

The current landscape contains numerous examples of "social cooperatives" that embody the co-op conception of value. These are co-ops in sectors such as health care, eldercare, social services, and workforce integration (helping people with disabilities, the unemployed, migrants, and those with criminal records find employment). Work in these sectors is often grueling and physically demanding, and the benefits of a cooperatively organized care sector quickly blend with those of other SDGs: health and well-being. Research shows that co-op members in care sectors are more likely to proactively care for their own health. "Members of a co-op get sick less often, and when they do get sick, they are more likely to get treatment and they seek treatment earlier than people who aren't in co-ops," Daniel Cahill, of Equal Care Cooperative in the UK, told me.[38] "I'm working for the co-op for thirty hours a week now. I used to work for another care provider for fifty to sixty hours a week." (Increased self-care is also a factor in cooperative sectors outside of care. As Marjorie Kelly points out, women in co-ops are more likely to get prenatal, postnatal, and delivery care, because members of co-ops are protected from large expenditures on health care and the need to take on crushing health-related debt.[39])

Multi-stakeholder social cooperatives are another site of care. They are particularly widespread in Italy—where the model was invented in the 1970s—and account for 15,000 of that country's co-ops. Multi-stakeholder social cooperatives include workers, consumers, producers, and often the local community in their ownership and governance, frequently concentrating on delivering care-related goods or services. With an average size of just thirty members, Italian social cooperatives provide "sheltered employment" and services for nearly 7 million Italians. If they survive their first five years of existence, they are highly durable, with a survival rate of 80 percent.[40]

Italy's social co-ops "produce a lot of social innovation, not electronic innovation," the historian Vera Negri Zamagni told me in a video conference in the middle of the pandemic. "They are innovative in the sense that they bring care services to populations that are usually underserved. Young children, older people, people with disabilities such as autism, but also migrants, and former prisoners. People with disabilities are employed successfully in restaurants as waiters. Italians love that kind of inclusion. Multi-stakeholder co-ops are more agile than many government programs."[41]

Another form of often care-based multi-stakeholder co-ops is the community cooperative. These are stakeholder cooperatives that have emerged as bottom-up initiatives for the preservation, use, and regeneration of community assets, as well as the management of quasi-public services and community development projects.[42] While both multi-stakeholder social cooperatives and community cooperatives have many stakeholder groups and are frequently focused on serving the needs of a specific community, community cooperatives often have a broader range of stakeholders, which can extend as far as all residents of a small town. They have become increasingly common in the aging, lightly populated villages of the Italian Alps. They are not specialized in any one thing; they may cut timber in the woods, run a restaurant, or operate the post office or hotel.

Evolving Configurations That Support Artists

For generations, artists have joined together to amplify their collective voice. Charlie Chaplin and a group of fellow filmmakers became a symbol of collective power in 1919 when they formed United Artists, a profound break from the control asserted by traditional commercial studios. This is without a doubt one of the most iconic examples of artists working together for a common cause. Long before multinational conglomerates owned the movie industry, these creatives believed in finding valuable autonomy through solidarity. Fast-forwarding to 1947, Robert Kappa, Henri Cartier-Bresson, and a cohort of photographers strove to create Magnum Photos, an international enterprise designed to disrupt the photography industry and guarantee collective support for their craft. Now Magnum has offices all over the world—from New York City to Tokyo—and continues to keep the cooperative spirit alive.

In the twenty-first century, musicians have received only 12 percent of total revenues flowing through the music industry. Spotify, a publicly traded streaming platform with more than 25 million artists and 140 million subscribers, provides easy access to music and has a market capitalization of $48 billion. But the artists featured on the platform earn less than half a cent per stream—a song must be played 250 times for them to earn one dollar.[43] Black-boxed algorithmic curation systems, meanwhile, recommend customized music to listeners. According to one study, just 0.4 percent of Spotify's artists receive at least 10 percent of the company's royalties.[44] As of this writing, there are no artists on Spotify's board of directors.

Clearly, a stakeholder-owned music-streaming platform could address the need for more equitable profit distribution, but it doesn't have to compete with Spotify directly. Instead, an ecosystem of smaller companies adhering to cooperative principles and sharing digital infrastructure can provide alternatives to marketplace-dominating venture-backed platforms.

To see what artist ownership of streaming platforms might look like, let us turn to three existing small-scale, musician-run cooperatives that prioritize communal, social, and human capital over capitalism: Catalytic Sound, Ampled, and Resonate.

Catalytic Sound, like an indie record store in a world dominated by big-box retailers, is a "collective of creative musicians in more control of the dissemination and sale of their available discographies." Put simply, 50 percent of the money spent at Catalytic Sound goes directly to musicians. One article describes Catalytic Sound as "an organization that aspires to anarchic egalitarianism, with each member given a voice in every institutional decision . . . For artists, this means the financial security to spend time working on and developing their artistic practice—not hours at day jobs."[45] Catalytic Sound, with a modest subscriber base of 141 (and counting), uses the digital infrastructure of Patreon, SoundCloud, and BandCamp to host and stream music.

Ampled is a New York–based platform cooperative with more than 500 artists that, in the words of its founders, "is 100 percent owned, controlled, and governed by its artists, workers, and community [and] provides a service for artists as a response to failures of industry incumbents to meet artist needs."[46] The owners control how they produce, market, and sell their music, and in the process create a sustaining culture of appreciation and support.

The co-op offers various classes, including one for producer members (artists who have pages with more than ten supporters), worker members (contributors who have put in at least eighty hours of work), and community members who pay the community membership fee. No member gets more than one vote. Ampled is built for sustainability and community benefit rather than for quick profits or the chance of being acquired by a bigger tech company. "We've become digital neoserfs—tilling on land we don't own, and giving our harvest away," said Ampled co-founder Austin Robey.[47] Unlike platforms such as Patreon, Ampled gives artist-members financial and decision-making power. Decisions touching on business strategy—such as approval of investment and fundraising strategies, redistribution of surplus, budgeting, and the approval of new contributors (artists)—are democratically made according to a system transparently explained on Ampled's website.[48]

As a pioneering arts collective, Ampled defines the value that they see in their co-op in multiple ways: collective ownership, participatory and democratic governance, and eventually an equitable approach to the sharing of material reward.

Ampled invites artists and supporters to audit their financial decisions on its website and is developing a governance token system for its 'Time Bank,' which will allow contributing members to work for Ampled for a few hours and then receive services from other members for the same amount of time.

The third arts collective showing the way forward is Resonate, a music-streaming platform co-op with a community of 30,000 people.[49] "Our community represents music for people that actually care about music," Rich Jensen, Resonate's chief executive, explained to me. "I call it the vast minority, which might be only half of 1 percent of the population, the people [for whom] music is their superpower."[50] Resonate transcends the label of "Spotify killer" and embarks on its own unique path, offering a captivating musical voyage that deeply resonates with devoted listeners.

As with the others, Resonate's platform co-op is well suited to the music industry because it fosters genuine communities of artists, fans, designers, and technologists. The fact that its musician listings are not manipulated by opaque algorithms—and its listeners are not mined by surveillance technologies—only adds to the value that such platform co-ops provide. And even if

Ampled, Catalytic Sound, and Resonate do not guarantee living wages for their artists, what they do offer sure beats Spotify.

Bringing Value to Rural Communities

There's a form of value creation often overlooked in assessments of cooperatives: preservation of rural traditions. Cooperative values in the agricultural sector in Brazil preserve rural traditions and account for approximately 64 percent of the sector's revenue, making it a promising area for platform cooperatives to reach younger generations and provide new opportunities.[51] This includes everything from small family farms to large-scale commercial operations. Aline Augusta de Oliveira, a young co-op employee, told me at the biggest conference of a national cooperative association, Sistema OCB in Brasília, that she saw value to "the rural" as the biggest potential for platform co-ops. "Platform co-ops can reach our generation in rural areas and give us new opportunities," she said.

The value that platform co-ops can bring to rural and suburban communities is seen clearly in the work of Mobicoop, a rideshare co-op that collaborates with rural French municipalities to solve the "last mile problem." Mobi offers an alternative source of income for drivers and provides a platform co-op template that can be adopted by local municipalities and integrated with their train system, allowing commuters to arrange transportation from the train to their home with competitive pay rates.

We Own the Story

In November 1999, while teaching at a university in Portland, Oregon, I organized a bus to take my students to Seattle for the street protests against the World Trade Organization. During these protests, remembered today as "The Battle of Seattle," a new media organization called Indymedia was established. The activist publishing platform was launched to counter mainstream coverage of the protests that—if history was any guide—was sure to be sensationalist, superficial, and antagonistic, deploying a journalistic frame that emphasized violence over discussion of the reasons for the protest and its political agenda. Based largely on the market failure of corporate news at the local and national level, Indymedia's value proposition was straightforward: to tell the story of the protests from a grassroots perspective using Web 2.0, meaning that YOU, YES YOU, could also write the news.

At the time, it was called "read/write technology." Along with other citizen journalism platforms such as Protest.net, Paper Tiger TV, or Deep Dish TV, the shoestring broadsheet and network of journalists became critically important just a few years later during the run-up to the US-led invasion of Iraq, when *The New York Times* and other major media propagated the obvious lies of the Bush administration about the existence of weapons of mass destruction.

The behavior of papers like the *Times* before, during, and after the invasion of Iraq was fully in line with that predicted by Noam Chomsky's landmark 1988 analysis of US corporate mass media, co-authored with Edward S. Herman, *Manufacturing Consent*. The work describes such media in the United States as "effective and powerful ideological institutions that carry out a system-supportive propaganda function, by reliance on market forces, internalized assumptions, and self-censorship, and without overt coercion," using the propaganda model of communication.[52]

By contrast, the country's independent news outlets, such as Indymedia, and voices in the emergent blogosphere pointed out that there was no clear evidence for these weapons of mass destruction. This, too, was in line with analysis showing that news organizations owned by all their stakeholders—counting employees, journalists, and readers—contribute diversity to the media landscape and provide more accountability in the form of a willingness to challenge official narratives handed down from political and economic elites.[53]

This kind of value creation has a long history in US media and around the world. The cooperative model for media has a long history, including the formation of the Associated Press (AP) in 1846 by four New York City daily newspapers to cover the Mexican-American War and compete with sensationalist penny presses. The AP provided exclusive news to its members and charged newspapers based on usage, becoming a major news provider for papers across the US.

Efsyn (2015), a media cooperative in Greece, is among notable cooperatives in journalism such as *New Internationalist* (1973), *Il Manifesto* (1969), *Die Wochenzeitung* (1984), *Médor* (2015), *Positive News* (1993), *La Jornada* (1984), *Die Tageszeitung* (1991), and *Alternativas Económicas* (2013).

Cooperative ownership has long had a presence in journalism, but in the digital age it offers new ways to create value and defend against censorship, with platform co-ops being better suited for protecting reader privacy and using distributed technologies to make it harder to shut down dissident journalism websites. Blockchain technology also has potential use cases, and media cooperatives can adopt locally appropriate versions of the multi-stakeholder cooperative model, involving the broader community in the organization.

As this model is developed, there will be failures to learn from. One such case involved Civil Media Company, a ConsenSys-backed company that described itself as "the decentralized marketplace for sustainable journalism."[54] Civil sought to use a native cryptocurrency called the CVL token to nurture and defend the independence of public journalism, but its fundraising fell far short of its goal, and the vast majority of tokens were purchased by ConsenSys, thereby centralizing a purportedly decentralized

governance system.[55] In 2020, after two years of operation, the
project closed down.[56] Civil followed in the footsteps of the Banyan
Project, which was founded by journalist Tom Stites as an early
attempt to support reader-owned, local news cooperatives and to
combat the trend of "news deserts" around the world.

Rethinking Value Creation

Let's close by returning to Tyler Cowen's curt dismissal of co-ops,
large and small, during our encounter in Madrid as "too marginal
to consider." As I have shown, such dismissal requires genuine
tunnel vision regarding the value generated by co-ops. But his
comment got me thinking.

A more comprehensive perspective might acknowledge and
value the fact that cooperatives create multiple forms of value for
workers, communities, and the economy that are barely reflected
in GDP. Traditional worker cooperatives spread a culture of
human dignity, contribute to the education of their members, and
pay their employees fairly.

A clear picture of this emerges from the work of British economist Virginie Pérotin, who has conducted extensive research on
worker cooperatives and, as I mentioned earlier, found them to be
more productive than traditional firms.[57] Pérotin attributes this
greater productivity to three key factors: workers are more attached
to their organization, they have higher levels of trust, and they
exchange knowledge more effectively. This leads to workers feeling more invested in the business and more likely to go above and
beyond their job description. The result is a virtuous cycle of trust
and buy-in that results in greater stability, security, and motiv-
ation for workers—and more productivity for the firm.

Cooperatives create jobs for marginalized groups, facilitate
care for children and the elderly, and promote workplace democracy to raise expectations and encourage political participation.

They also contribute to the UN's Sustainable Development Goals by promoting intersectionality, Indigenous justice, and support for rural values.

Co-op advocates tout these forms of value in aggregate as having "social impact," but such impact is also in the particular, and can be described as returning "dignity" to labor and life. In this chapter, I quoted several workers who embody and demonstrate this lived dignity. Those who leave cooperatives often look for "co-opy" qualities in other jobs, even if the job market is tilted against them; if they don't find them, they are more likely to demand them.

Let's turn to the unique forms of value creation—realized and potential—found in the cooperative digital economy. I believe that it is here, in contrast to the mainstream "glamour" platforms, that co-op models offer underappreciated social and economic value propositions for start-up entrepreneurs and users.

Platform co-ops provide self-organization and autonomy, offering an open digital social economy that begins in the workplace. They maintain control over user and worker data, promote a commons-oriented approach, and facilitate democratic decision-making and control within distributed ownership structures, allowing workers to escape "the algorithmic bosses."

As we saw in the case of Up & Go, platform co-ops can offer higher pay—at times double or more the market rate—and more freedom and security. Members of Equal Care describe the joys of being able to organize their own time and have a better work-life balance, and of being relieved of the paperwork that defined their former jobs. The members of Mobicoop in France echoed the sentiments of the young woman at the Brazilian Co-op Conference I mentioned earlier, regarding the potential in rural areas. In particular, they saw the value of solving "the last mile problem." Food delivery platforms like Consegne Etiche in Bologna are using bicycles to promote ecological sustainability, while

Brazil's Cataki is helping disadvantaged recyclers locate recyclable material. Cooperatives prioritize the stability of all stakeholders over short-term profits, making them more successful in times of crisis. Platform cooperatives illustrate that a people-centered gig economy is not some far-off fantasy but is manifested by owner-workers on a daily basis, at work and at rest.

5

Roots of Resilience:
Unions and Platform Cooperatives

I paid a visit to Mensakas, a Catalonian cooperative food delivery app, at their headquarters on the second floor of Via Laietana in Barcelona. The modernist architecture and proximity to the Ramblas draw locals and visitors to the avenue, which runs from Plaça Urquinaona to Plaça d'Antonio López by the seafront. I walked up a stairwell beside a small supermarket, knocked on the door of Intersindical Alternativa de Catalunya, a self-described "militant, independent alliance" of Catalonian unions, and then walked through tall, heavy wooden doors, where one of Mensakas's founders, Oriol, a gentle man in his late twenties greeted me warmly.

Oriol told me about how former UberEats, Glovo, and Deliveroo couriers banded together in 2017 to fight "for labor rights and decent living conditions for home delivery workers, as well as the future of the working class as a whole."[1]

Against the sounds of the city at midday, Oriol recounted in detail the co-op's origin story, beginning with the frustrations of local couriers working for UberEats, Deliveroo, and Glovo. Angry about their low wages and lack of rights, they joined together to fight for something better, something they could control. As Oriol told this story, we were joined by one of those original couriers, Txiki Blasi, who proudly revealed that his group of Deliveroo couriers took the lead in developing the platform co-op that became Mensakas. "We are working-class people!" Blasi exclaimed.

Their first step was to join a courier association called Riders X Derechos (Riders4Rights). A year later, the eventual founders of Mensakas joined the Intersindical Alternativa de Catalunya. Together, they decided to strike against Deliveroo. The strike involving 200 couriers successfully pressured the company to change its contracts, but unfortunately, it made it difficult for the Mensakas founders to continue working with Deliveroo. The couriers then took Deliveroo to court, forcing the company to hire them as full-time employees. Deliveroo, ironically, offered them jobs in the company's Outreach division, which of course they declined. This turn of events proved that union-led work stoppages, while possibly useful for gaining leverage, can also have inconsistent outcomes for workers. Indeed, even "successful strikes" do not always produce workplace power, workplace control, or structural power in the way that cooperative bylaws, ownership rights, and decision-making authority do.

To get by, the targeted couriers established the platform co-op Mensakas the following May. Mensakas has sought to make the promise "Be your own boss" a reality—unlike the big platforms, which simply rehash it as empty marketing rhetoric. With Mensakas, workers set their own hours, control the digital platform, and keep the profits. They are using software from CoopCycle, a French member-governed association that represents and supports worker cooperatives for couriers across Europe, and beyond, with fleet management, restaurant management software, and external integration with third-party software. Together with the platform co-op model, the affiliated union was always part of Mensakas's project.

When thinking of unions, many people imagine factory workers bargaining for better wages and benefits, represented by union officials. Mensakas shows how unions and co-ops can and should work together in the platform economy. It demonstrates that unions are not, as some might think, expandable in the cooperative context. Indeed, this chapter highlights the advantages that can come from collaborations between traditional unions and platform cooperatives.

Historically, beginning in their shared cradle in the north of England in the 1840s, unions and co-ops have developed as the two organizational structures dedicated to helping workers. Indeed, early in their history, they were interchangeable. In Victorian England, all forms of worker self-organization, including co-ops, were commonly referred to as "unions" or "friendly societies." Pioneering theorists of cooperativism, such as Beatrice and Sidney Webb, were also among the co-founders of the London School of Economics and Political Science and wrote extensively about unions and other forms of collective action.

Against the reality of a long-term decline in trade union membership, it is more important than ever for unions and co-ops to remember this shared history, pool their assets, and once again merge their strengths to improve the situation of workers everywhere. Unions, despite experiencing a decline in many industrialized countries, still have significant revenue, societal power to change discourse through "boots on the ground" in traditional industries, and a deep connection to large numbers of workers in most countries. They also have physical spaces, organizational skills, and long-standing relationships with policymakers. To these institutional assets, co-ops—and platform co-ops in particular—bring their own unique contributions, not the least of which are access to workers in nonunionized sectors and expertise in the realities of life in the gig economy. For these and other reasons, I believe the modern labor movement's traditional reservations of co-ops—especially regarding their ability to enforce collective bargaining agreements—is not only misplaced, but increasingly anachronistic.

Organizing without Bosses

Due to the blurred lines between employee and owner in co-ops, member-owners may not have fully grasped the advantages that a conventional union can offer, or may not have been motivated to pursue them. Most people in English-speaking countries and their colonies view the union as having an adversarial relationship with management while also second-guessing worker ownership. Without those distinctions and conflicting interests to provide the overarching structural dynamic, what's the point?

There are good reasons for thinking that co-ops and unions are contradictory models for creating worker power. Unions are typically seen within the co-op movement as top-down organizations, with a small group of leaders making decisions that affect the entire membership. In contrast, cooperatives are owned and controlled by their workers, giving everyone an equal say in how the business is run. Cooperative enterprises may have reservations about unions, as they could potentially disrupt the decision-making processes, implying the presence of internal conflicts, and introduce unnecessary costs through union dues, along with concerns about external control over their operations. While the models of unions and cooperatives may seem different at first glance, there are many underlying similarities. Unions advocate for the rights of workers both within and outside of businesses, while cooperatives inherently involve workers in the solutions from the outset due to their ownership structure. Crucially, both types of organization rely on the power of solidarity.

The skepticism cuts both ways. As the British trade unionist David O'Connell explained to me, unions are often remarkably apprehensive about claims that the cooperative movement can build class solidarity. A common union view, he points out, "is that a cooperative business may do wonderful things for its owners or users, but it will simply want to make a profit, and wouldn't necessarily mobilize them to take action in support of workers in another part of the industry."[2] It is a frequently leveled criticism that worker cooperatives serve as an "exit-gateway" from class conflict and consciousness, an alternative to class struggle that entices workers to participate in the capitalist system, albeit on their own terms.[3] Beatrice and Sidney Webb leveled one objection against cooperatives, arguing that instead of workers organizing to fight and win, they become "petty capitalists." As the unions frequently expressed it, cooperatives "seek to build and develop a tiny slice of capital outside of the direct control of big industrialists. In other words, cooperatives retreat from the direct struggle between workers and owners."[4]

Unions within worker-owned businesses, which can serve as "legitimate opposition" according to one scholar, can also meaningfully represent nonmembers of a co-op, thus providing reasons why co-ops open their doors to unions. But there are many reasons why such syndicates make sense.[5]

Take, for instance, this story of a coal mine in Wales. A 2001 study compared the results of its dispute-resolution processes when operated by a Welsh cooperative compared with those used by the British government.[6] The story began when 237 employees purchased a Welsh coal mine from British Coal and converted it into the Tower Colliery cooperative. Opting for union representation, motivated workers in 1995 chose to pay their redundancy costs to support a buyout scheme offered by the union, rather than risking unemployment.

The cooperative was now mandated to hire managers in charge of safety, finance, engineering, and other roles. But the board of directors retained the power to overrule the decisions of these managers. Historically, disputes at the government-owned mine were routinely confrontational and settled through procedures resulting in work stoppages. Yet, under cooperative management, the process became shorter and more flexible, lowering the level of conflict. Tower Colliery was 100 percent worker-owned and -operated like a cooperative, although being technically registered as a private limited company. In contrast to British Coal, which frequently experienced grievances or union action, conflicts at Tower Colliery were less severe, and the workers, who were now also owners, worked harder. The more balanced power dynamic between workers and managers resulted in a more amicable and collegial style of management.

Tower Colliery, operating with a shareholder democracy and complete union representation, remained profitable until the mine was depleted in 2008.

A limitation in the union argument against cooperatives is the habitual conjecture that cooperative forms are homogeneous and exclusively serve their workers while neglecting problems of running a business. Critics may want to consider multi-stakeholder cooperatives, geared toward meeting the needs of producers, workers, and the larger community, with social co-ops being a subset of these coops that focus on delivering social services. These are distinct from traditional cooperatives in that they have a specific social mission, which can include everything from providing affordable housing to providing services for people with disabilities. Social cooperatives can be found the world over, often organized under cooperative federations that connect and support their work. They can grow from the soil of any number of local political traditions and cultures.

In Italy, the government's reduced national budget for the welfare system (a real-terms cut of 13 percent between 2008 and 2011) prompted citizens to self-organize and provide essential-care services. The government assisted this process by enacting laws to support multi-stakeholder cooperatives. Consortia of Italian social cooperatives have allowed this model to be scaled to a point where it can compete with larger corporations. Nevertheless, despite progress, social disparities persist in Italy, as the number of individuals living in "absolute poverty" has significantly increased sicne 2008, with 32.4 percent being noncitizens and 7.2 percent being citizens.[7]

Cooperatives have a legacy of employing differently abled workers, engaging broader communities, and acting as custodians of the urban commons. Citizens in Perugia, a city between Rome and Florence, established a community cooperative to acquire a decommissioned "postmodernissimo" cinema. Aside from running the cinema as a business, the goal was to revitalize a section of town desolated by rising crime. The cinema evolved into a meeting place and cultural center, a model for urban renewal. Residents of Perugia refer to the cinema as their "city commons." They are in charge of what happens there. One section is designated for families with infants and nursing mothers.

The union critique further ignores the important contribution co-ops can make in organizing exploited gig workers. "In most countries, the existing trade union movement lacks effective strategies to organize gig workers," note the British scholars Jamie Woodcock and Mark Graham.[8] Indeed, as one union organizer put it to me, "Private-sector unions have dismal density, and public-sector unions are not faring much better. If unions can't solve labor's woes, it may not be simply because organized labor is dying, but because organized labor needs to change."[9]

It is hardly a secret that trade unions have struggled to adapt to deindustrialization and the rise of gig and service economies in the twenty-first century. Gig workers operate in a deregulated environment defined by an entirely new type of employment. Woodcock and Graham emphasize that with the rise of the gig economy, workplace risk has shifted from the employer to the isolated, nonunionized worker with little leverage or legal standing. The gig economy, for all its technological wonders, has turned the clock back on labor conditions and workplace protections.[10]

Work in the gig economy is characterized by its high intensity, low pay, unpredictable hours, arbitrary firing, and isolating nature, while also leaving workers vulnerable to harassment and without formal channels for filing complaints about their situation. Organizing these sectors can be resource-intensive and yield a low return on investment for unions. For this reason, many unions in developed countries prefer to focus on traditional employment relations in large, established firms. When I asked about organizing delivery drivers under platform co-ops, one German union official disparagingly responded, "But that's not what unions do."

For workers facing this dismal picture, the unionized platform co-op offers an effective model for modern workplace struggle. It is not just ragtag couriers who have come to realize this. Forward-thinking legacy unions, such as California's Service Employees International Union—United Healthcare Workers West (SEIU-UHW), which brought together "100,000 health-care workers, patients, and consumers to ensure affordable, accessible, high-quality care for all Californians," have begun to reintroduce union cooperatives.[11]

But what about more tectonic events and alliances capable of pulling together the might and milieus of labor and the co-op movement? Is it possible to conceive of a gig-economy version of the 1912 Lawrence Textile strike? This strike, led by the Industrial Workers of the World (IWW) in defense of mostly female textile workers, involved more than 20,000 people—a turnout previously unthinkable in that industry. Together with a growing number of labor activists, I believe that platforms like Freelance.com and UpWork—employing a combined 40 million people worldwide—make gig work a prime territory for mass-scale, international labor organizing.

Workers worldwide are exploring new ways to exercise their power through innovative labor models, such as the Independent Workers' Union of Great Britain (IWGB), a fully independent trade union founded in 2013 with eleven branches organizing low-wage London migrants to fight "gig economy" employment laws.

Beyond the IWGB, there is the International Alliance of App-Based Transport Workers (IAATW), which was founded in January 2020 by app-based drivers from sixteen countries and six continents. Workers from Uber, Lyft, Ola, Grab, and Didi, as well as other smaller companies, constitute this alliance. The union is dedicated to fighting for the rights of app-based transportation workers and improving driver working conditions.[12] The union is advancing driver rights and the dignity of the profession around the world by cooperating across political, geographic, and company boundaries to support drivers and other app-based transportation workers.

These are just the most visible of a number of experiments with associational worker power taking place throughout the United Kingdom, Germany, Georgia, India, Bangladesh, France, the Netherlands, and Italy.[13] Unions often overlook the creative and urgent efforts of gig workers due to the belief that organizing them is too difficult and not worth their resources. This traditional approach, however, no longer works in the gig economy, where workers are dispersed and may not be able or willing to pay union dues. Unions need to adapt to the changing landscape and find new ways to organize and support workers in the gig economy.

Luckily, technologies and organizing models are emerging that will allow for sectoral organizing of gig economy workers. They combine in the platform co-op, a structure capable of uniting and pooling a geographically dispersed workforce. The digital co-op is the modern-day factory canteen.

AlliedUP

The caregiving industry is one of the industries of the future. The World Health Organization predicts that the number of people aged eighty and up will triple between 2020 and 2050, requiring a huge increase in professional caregivers in both residential and hospital settings.[14] To keep up with rising demand, the United States alone will need to hire at least 200,000 nurses each year.[15]

Even so, caregiving work is currently structured to be low-paying, often demeaning, and devoid of social capital. More broadly, according to a recent survey, nearly 30 percent of health-care professionals in the United States are thinking about leaving their jobs.[16] The COVID-19 pandemic was a contributing factor—by the middle of November 2020, 22 percent of US hospitals were experiencing staffing shortages—but it was far from the only one. Can cooperative communities provide viable alternatives to exploitative gig-work platforms and chronic-care facilities, and thus solve one of the great social crises of the coming decades?

One organization wrestling with this and related questions is the SEIU-UHW, the 100,000-member health-care workers' union in California.[17] At an accelerating pace since the start of the pandemic, the SEIU-UHW—representing frontline caregivers such as respiratory-care practitioners and dietary, janitorial, and nursing staff—has begun experimenting with a union-cooperative staffing model that can address turnover rates as well as quality-of-care issues like patient wait times.

Along with representing its members in labor disputes and bargaining, the SEIU-UHW assists health-care workers in starting their own businesses, on the premise that people know best what is good for them. "This is the first time that our union has had a worker-cooperative partner . . . we had to be slow and careful in a way we couldn't be with a different employer," says Ra Criscitiello, research coordinator at SEIU-UHW West. "The union has a collective bargaining agreement with the co-op [that in some respects is] more collaborative than any other relationship the union has."[18]

In January 2016, the SEIU-UHW launched NursesCan to address a number of organizational challenges, from supporting licensed vocational nurses (LVNs) in negotiations with hospitals to fighting hospitals' relentless outsourcing to nonunion staffing agencies (a practice in violation of the California Board of Accountancy rules). The experimental project started small: twenty-two unionized nurses were given an app to schedule home visits and become co-owners as well as employees. Out of this successful pilot grew the NursesCan platform cooperative, which is now used by St. John's Well-Child and Family Center Clinics in Los Angeles to provide on-demand and at-home care. Along with the assistance of the SEIU-UHW, the NursesCan platform cooperative has benefited from the aid of a professional business developer.

As a union alternative to non-worker-centered on-demand staffing agencies, the local envisioned a unionized co-op of licensed vocational nurses. Dr. Helen Duplessis, chief medical officer at St. John's, said:

> Home visits by NursesCan LVNs have extended our available resources for rendering needed services to pregnant women. The home visits provide a welcome alternative to office-based visits for pregnant women who certainly benefit from the health education and psycho-social support, but don't always have the time to make it back to the clinic for all of the interventions that are ideal during their pregnancy.[19]

The co-op-provided licensed vocational nurses are ideal for home visits because they can provide a broader range of care at a lower cost than a physician or registered nurse; additionally, they can be remotely monitored. Hospitals and clinics, according to

Criscitiello, want to use on-demand staff more frequently and will respond positively to the unionized platform co-op model.[20] The co-op has also delivered an unexpected benefit: patient no-show rates at clinics dropped significantly.

In California, the SEIU-UHW now has working relationships with more than 6,000 licensed vocational nurses. If the need arises, additional LVNs can be trained and licensed in less than two years. In just a few years, Criscitiello expects thousands of union health-care professionals working in co-ops to deliver millions of visits to hospitals and clinics. As a related matter, the cooperative model allows the union to address staffing issues by reaching out to part-time, nonunionized workers.[21]

People learning about this model may find it confusing at first. Why would a worker cooperative require a union when the workers are also the owners of the cooperative? Are they expected to sit in a room and bargain with themselves? Because unionized cooperatives such as NursesCan are not adversarial employers, the SEIU-UHW uses a very general, short collective bargaining agreement for them. In addition, when a co-op grows, a union can help monitor and guarantee the welfare of its extended workforce. Importantly, because of its size, the SEIU-UHW is able to provide benefits to small cooperatives they would not be able to obtain on their own. From the union's perspective, this also ensures that co-ops implement industry-standard pay, eliminating the risk that they will undercut unionized enterprises.

In March 2021, the SEIU-UHW built on the success of Nurses-Can by establishing AlliedUP, a much larger staffing co-op that serves "allied health-care staff," or care workers who are not nurses or physicians. AlliedUP offers health-care staffing on a full-time, part-time, and temporary-assignment basis, allowing employees to schedule shifts that fit their schedules. AlliedUP focuses on five of California's largest metropolitan areas, which often suffer shortages of allied health professionals. The group currently has nearly fifty worker-owners placed at hospitals and clinics across California, and features a governance structure that maximizes transparency within the company.

Five of the worker-owners are on the Worker Ownership Committee, which encourages collective entrepreneurship and enhances worker voice and influence. Members of the committee co-develop policies and practices that build a strong and worker-centered ownership culture, reinforced by a team of national worker cooperative experts. Because AlliedUP workers are spread across the state, worker-owner meetings, including the Worker Ownership Committee's, are held in the evening and use interactive tools like Miro boards and video-conferencing.

There are several key differences between the AlliedUP cooperative model and the traditional low-wage health-care staffing model. Licensed vocational nurses earn an average of $35 per hour with AlliedUP, which is more than $4 more per hour than the traditional staffing model. Compared with traditional allied health staffing organizations, AlliedUP now offers not only competitive compensation but also better benefits, such as employer-funded medical, dental, and vision insurance, paid time off, and educational opportunities.[22] The collective bargaining agreement between AlliedUP and the SEIU-UHW gives AlliedUP workers access to the union's large education fund, which provides upskilling, apprenticeship, and career-ladder programs that lead to significant wage growth.

For example, Dianne Ocampo, a medical assistant at Kaiser Permanente Redwood City, received support from multiple education fund programs for different forms of continuing education, including coursework at San Francisco State University and a local community college, where she ultimately earned an associate's degree in nursing. She graduated from both programs with honors and was accepted into the New Grad RN residency program in Northern California. "The cooperative rewards higher education with higher pay. Such extraordinary benefits are simply not available to nonunion gig workers who are classified as independent contractors," Ocampo shared.[23]

AlliedUP is designed to address another issue in the gig economy: how to pay workers benefits even if they work for multiple hospitals or other clients.

"When you think of a staffing company, the only benefit that you can think of is the job itself," explains Verenice Rodriguez, a medical assistant who is one of the co-op's owners. "With AlliedUP, you have job flexibility, medical benefits, and a 401(k), to name a few benefits. Not having to work 40 hours a week and still being able to qualify for medical benefits will make a huge difference to me and my family."

AlliedUP aims to employ more than 2,000 benefited, well-paid caregivers by 2024, and as of this writing seems to be on track. They've raised significant capital and have contracts with six large hospital and clinic systems. But while it appears to be a promising model for the United States' overall broken health-care system, one can't help but wonder if it might not create a part-time cooperative alternative at the expense of building a more stable system of full-time, long-term work.

Women of color account for up to 76 percent of allied health-care workers. In a more just society, those women would be educated and paid to become fully trained nurses with full-time union jobs, ideally employed by hospitals with strong legacy collective bargaining agreements. It is better to prioritize the education and compensation of more full-time nurses and doctors over early-career personnel, and one possible solution to this issue is AlliedUP's collaboration with two large education funds, which aims to advance low-wage healthcare workers into higher-wage positions, such as registered nurses.

Despite these nuances, the model of a unionized platform cooperative holds the promise of connecting workers and allowing them to jointly make decisions, providing access to better benefits, educating their members so that they can find better paying jobs, and matching patients with local, licensed vocational nurses. AlliedUp is currently developing a digital platform to realize and extend the frontier of the model's potential. As a pioneer and success story, it is a gig economy co-op to watch in the years to come.

The Ghost of the Knights of Labor

The Korean government passed the Framework Act on Cooperatives, which went into force on December 1, 2012, to allow platform workers to create platform cooperatives but not unionize. This was a significant victory for the Korean cooperative movement. The act established a general cooperative law covering worker and freelancer cooperatives, which had previously been regulated by eight distinct cooperative laws. The act also provided a range of incentives for cooperative formation and development, such as tax breaks and access to government funding.

At 4 a.m. on December 2, the night after the Framework passed into law, one group of transport workers then and there established a platform cooperative called the Association of Alternate Drivers.[24] In South Korea, "alternate drivers" are people who can drive your car for you when you're too drunk to drive yourself home. Alternate drivers are especially useful in countries like Korea where public transportation is not always reliable or convenient. The association had spent two years organizing drivers in anticipation of this law, using an internet café as a meeting place; now that the organization was official, it could get right to work.

After the Framework Act passed, the 22 owners and 693 associated members of the alternate driver co-op acted like a traditional union by educating members on their rights and advocating for them with policymakers. They convinced Seoul's government to build a rest facility for co-op workers, and by 2018, the Korean government opened four more facilities for these workers, a significant achievement after being previously overlooked.

Nearly 6,900 miles away, the Drivers Cooperative in New York City is bringing together taxi and delivery drivers committed to improving the industry (introduced in chapter 1). It is thriving thanks to its success in improving driver pay and working conditions and providing new-driver training and support. The Drivers Cooperative's success has been aided by the strong grassroots presence and inspirational model of robust local labor organizations and traditions. In New York City, taxi workers are organized into several unions that have long advocated for their rights and improvement of working conditions. The largest and most influential is the New York Taxi Workers Alliance, founded in 1998, which represents 25,000 New York City yellow cab, green car, black car, livery, and app-dispatched drivers. The worker advocacy group and self-identified union has been instrumental in winning workers important benefits and protections. Another active union is the Independent Driver Guild (IDG), which represents more than 65,000 for-hire car drivers in New York City. IDG has a process in place for members to protest being barred from using the platform.[25] Significantly, Uber funds the IDG and has the authority to pick the drivers serving on the appeals panel. Drivers Co-op, by contrast, has a "jury of drivers' peers," which is a platform co-op conflict resolution council that helps resolve disputes between drivers and the co-op.[26]

The New York City and South Korean drivers' associations demonstrate how the gig economy has necessitated and birthed new approaches to associational worker power—and how platforms can lead the way. But although the technologies enabling the union-cooperative hybrid are new, the basic idea is not. In the decades following the Civil War in the United States, cooperative stores and factories flourished. At the center of this meshing were the Knights of Labor (KOL), an American labor federation that peaked in the 1880s with about 1 million members in the United States, Canada, and, to a lesser extent, Australia and the United Kingdom.[27] According to co-op scholar John Curl's excellent book *For All the People: Uncovering the Hidden History of Cooperation, Cooperative Movements, and Communalism in America*, its total membership made the Knights the largest labor organization of its time.[28] In the US, the federation supported small farmers, laborers, and African Americans in the rural Deep South, where Black members built cooperative villages.

Unlike the American Federation of Labor, the KOL was a diverse labor union open to all workers. They considered wage earners to be a class. The Knights lobbied politicians, went on strike, supported other radical social movements, and formed hundreds of cooperatives that doubled as local assemblies with significant autonomy from the union leadership. They believed that "cooperativism" was essential for securing equal rights, liberty, and the pursuit of happiness for workers. They believed that this system allowed workers to control their own destinies and improve their economic situation. Their goal was to establish co-op institutions that could eventually replace the wage system.

Union members also formed co-ops to find work during labor disputes, failed strikes, lockouts, or blacklisting. Sixty percent of the union dues collected by the Knights' General Assembly in 1880 were designated for cooperative development. Many workers had an almost religious faith that cooperatives were the vehicles that could free the working class from wage servitude and employment precarity.

At the height of the Knights' success, Minneapolis was the capital of cooperative activity and home to approximately thirty-five cooperative firms. These firms included barrel factories, print shops, a shirt factory, and a cigar factory. Their success was dependent on a network of mutually supportive organizations that helped with publicity, funding, organizing, recruiting, and daily encouragement. In Chicago, the Knights' female members established twenty cooperative garment factories that shared revenues equally and whose members worked no more than eight hours per day.

Before the 1940s, union movements in industrialized countries considered employee ownership a top priority, sometimes even more important than wages and working conditions. However, the idea of ownership was lost during the "postwar consensus," and unions chose to focus on collective bargaining within the existing system rather than tackling the complex issue of ownership. This was unfortunate, because cooperative ownership and collective bargaining are in fact highly compatible.

The KOL embodied progressive values in a variety of ways, including anticipating and paving the way for eight-hour workday legislation, fighting for the establishment of public utilities and equal pay, albeit with limited participation in decision-making bodies. In the late nineteenth century, Horace Greeley, the influential publisher of the *New York Tribune*, was a prominent voice in the American labor movement. He supported the KOL, which eventually became one of the country's most powerful unions.

Greeley was active in the decades leading up to the Gilded Age, a time known for its excessive wealth accumulation and greed and its promotion of laissez-faire. According to this doctrine, government intervention in society or the market only leads to corruption and inefficiency. This sort of thinking had influenced post–Civil War government policies regarding labor relations and Reconstruction. For instance, proponents of laissez-faire opposed government initiatives to regulate labor conditions or aid former slaves. Despite opposition to government intervention in labor relations, Greeley used his newspaper to support the KOL and their cause, contributing to the organization's success and its impact on workers' rights reform.

Victor Drury, a French immigrant and labor activist in Pittsburgh, believed that cooperative stores could help empower workers and create a more just society by selling products slightly above cost. If demand for these products was high enough, Drury thought it made sense for the stores to start producing them themselves. In his book *The Polity of the Labor Movement*, he wrote that if they sold enough bread and pastry, they should establish a bakery and call upon Trades' Unions to provide skilled men to direct these centers of production.[29] This revolutionary dream became a reality when members of the KOL created centers for production and employment that advanced their cooperative commonwealth. In the late 1800s, a member of KOL's board realized that it was impossible for cooperative units to reach their goals in large part because they were isolated within market economies. Therefore, it was imperative that the union build a self-sustaining cosmos of collaboration—a web of self-sufficient, self-governing, and self-employed cooperative communities. In 1883, the KOL national leadership backed a group of eight coal miners in leasing forty acres to establish a mine of their own, one link among many required for an overarching cooperative commonwealth. After it was outfitted, and railroad tracks laid to connect it to the main line nearby, the mine grew into the Knights' first active production cooperative.

There was just one problem: connecting the KOL experiment to the wider capitalist economy required cooperation that was not forthcoming. To transport their coal to market, the KOL mine required a connection between their tracks and the regional rail system; however, the local railroad corporation denied permission for such a connection. Unable to raise $4,000 to buy their own switch engine, the Knights were forced to sell the mine they had hoped might form the cornerstone of a national cooperative commonwealth.

The next major blow came in 1886, when a bomb exploded at a political rally in Haymarket Square in Chicago, killing several police officers and civilians. The KOL were blamed for the bombing, and the federation saw a major decline in membership. Many of its associated cooperatives were forced to close, as railroad companies, wholesalers, and banks initiated boycotts of them. At this point, numerous members of the KOL joined secret societies like the Industrial Workers of the World to persist in their struggle for labor rights and facilitate the emergence of the next generations of the cooperative movement.

Thanks to their efforts, workers today enjoy better wages, benefits, and working conditions. A KOL secretary named Davis Hanson Waite, who was elected governor of Colorado in 1893, formed the ruralist-populist People's Party with other American farmers. Before the year was over, Colorado became the second state to give women the right to vote.[30]

During its brief heyday, the KOL expanded the notion of the United States as a land of opportunity. They demanded dignity and empowerment not only for homestead farmers, but also for the men and women fighting for workplace democracy in the mines and the factories that were the lifeblood of the new industrial age. "The Knights of Labor connected workplace issues and labor rights with local, state, and federal policies, while actively engaging in politics, mutual aid, and economic development," explains American scholar Jessica Gordon Nembhard, underscoring the federation's enduring legacy and the interplay between the labor rights struggle and the pursuit of economic rights more broadly.[31]

In a similar way, platform co-ops can overhaul the union–co-op model for the digital age. Consider the case of workers categorized as independent contractors. The Maine Lobstering Union, known colloquially as IAM Lobster 207, was founded in 2013 by a group of Maine lobstermen. That year, in-season lobster prices had dropped to a twenty-year low of $1.80 per pound, leaving the workers, who are classified as independent contractors in Maine, in dire financial straits. Unable to pool their selling power to negotiate a better price, they were forced to accept the dockside price set by the wholesalers. These buyers were frequently representatives of large multinational companies that supplied seafood all over the world, but the lobstermen decided to fight for higher catch prices. The state industry's trade association, the Maine Lobster Association, served the interests of two groups with clashing interests: buyers and wholesalers, who wanted to buy at the lowest possible price, and lobstermen, who needed to make a living. When the lobstermen threatened to stop fishing until they got a fair selling price, the state responded by threatening an antitrust lawsuit against them. There was no clear path to economic justice.

In early 2013, several lobstermen in the town of Vinalhaven decided to seek advice from the Machinists Union. The union's staff members obliged and began organizing lobstermen, hosting gatherings for them to share their experiences and learn about union representation. By February of that year, ninety-nine lobstermen had signed A-cards and became Machinists members. The union invited a group of lobstermen to an educational retreat at the William W. Winpisinger Education and Technology Center in Maryland that spring. The trip was successful in fostering cooperation and collectivism among the newly organized lobstermen and the Machinists; it also helped the former develop a strategy for mobilizing and leveraging economic power. The lobstermen returned to Maine and became members of the Machinists under the newly formed Lobster 207 toward the end of 2013.

Lobster 207 members and Machinists continued their collaboration, and their researchers studied the possibility of forming a cooperative as a way to get around antitrust laws and allow lobstermen to pool their selling power as independent contractors. To this end, Lobster 207 members created a statewide lobster-marketing cooperative, with union lobstermen sharing profits from the Maine

Lobstering Union Co-op. This helped ballast the economic viability of lobstermen and their communities while prices remained low. At the same time, the union participated in environmental activities aimed at protecting lobsters, their habitat, and the ecosystem of the Maine coast.[32]

Lobster 207 showcases a distinctive approach to organizing independent contractors through a co-op, leveraging the power of association. This serves as an example of an innovative union–co-op model that can be tailored to the evolving ecosystem of platform co-ops.

The accomplishments of Lobster 207's cooperative model, in conjunction with its collaboration with the Machinists, serves as profound inspiration for the creation of inventive models of associational power that navigate the legal challenges inherent in conventional freelancing or independent contract work. Exploring formats like data cooperatives, data unions, and other collectives aids sustainable economic organization, helping workers in new sectors of the economy. Although the term "union" may not be entirely accurate in this context, as these models do not necessarily involve traditional labor organizing or collective bargaining, they still have the potential to become a powerful force for governance and possibly fairer compensation in the data economy. By sharing data and negotiating as a group, these organizations may achieve more equitable data arrangements, similar to how Lobster 207 members pooled their selling power as independent contractors.[33]

According to law professor Eric Posner and Microsoft researcher Glen Weyl, "data unions" that solicit members—the data laborers—by promising them higher payments for their data could approach Facebook or Google and threaten a "strike" (also, effectively, a boycott, because data laborers are simultaneously consumers of Facebook's and Google's services).[34] This ability to combine work stoppages with consumer boycotts sets them apart from traditional unions and can be used to create global public awareness of data production. Indeed, the concept of data, derived from the Latin word *datum*, meaning "something given," is interpreted and understood differently across various regions worldwide. Data gathering is not a top priority for many people focused on everyday survival. Data unions must therefore forge a direct connection between data democracy and the daily bread-and-butter struggles of the global labor movement.

Indeed, there are numerous instances where data cooperatives and unions have demonstrated effective collaboration. PROSA, a Danish IT union representing over 16,000 professionals, partnered with polypoly, a European data cooperative, to address the challenge of not wanting to host sensitive data such as salary information on their own servers. Polypoly's data wallet solution allows PROSA's members to securely store sensitive data on their own devices while maintaining employee privacy.

But while co-ops work toward the democratization of data, their promise shines brightest in recent examples of analog organizing, resistance, and reclamation. Of these, few are as powerful as the story of a worker-run window company on the South Side of Chicago, the longtime US capital of pioneering labor organizing.

I had discussed that the Knights of Labor established a network of female-run textile cooperatives in Chicago in the late nineteenth century; nearly 130 years later in the same city, history repeated itself when the New Era Windows Cooperative—represented today by the United Electrical Workers Union—was launched.

The story of New Era Windows began in 2008, when the Chicago-based company Republic Windows, hit hard by the global financial crisis, went bankrupt and closed its factory on the city's South Side for the first time in forty-three years of business. When Republic shut down, it left hundreds of workers without jobs. Faced with the prospect of unemployment, the workers decided to band together and purchase the factory. The efforts of Local 1110 members to keep the factory open provide a case study that can help unions develop strategies to support worker-led cooperative development. This is especially true of the union's powerful workplace occupation strategy, which won it the right of first refusal—the right that allows workers to buy a company before it's sold to others. Throughout the negotiations, union leadership deployed its members to maximize leverage, showing how union power can forge the steel needed to implement cooperative visions and build cooperative institutions.

This can also be seen in the case of the United Electrical Workers (UE). This union took a famously antagonistic stance on co-ops in the 1980s, rejecting horizontally organized cooperatives as a poor fit for union hierarchies. But when the 2008 financial crisis hit, the union began to see the cooperative as a novel strategy for reversing declines in membership and saving jobs. Following the effective transition of New Era Windows, the UE converted other workplaces into cooperatives. According to Brendan Martin, founder and president of the Working World, a nonprofit organization dedicated to providing financing and technical assistance to worker cooperatives both domestically and globally, unions can forge productive relationships with co-ops if they move beyond traditional bargaining units and instead focus on their broad mission of improving workers' well-being. The growing acceptance of unions partnering with cooperatives is reflected in the activities of several notable labor organizations.

In the United States, this is slowly becoming the conventional wisdom. The AFL-CIO and the SEIU officially promote the development of union cooperatives. Sweden has Unionen, a union committed to standardizing contracts for online businesses and helping unions and emerging platform co-ops develop new labor agreements and standardized regulations. Indeed, these dynamics are not confined solely to high-income countries but are unfolding in diverse regions across the globe.

SEWA: A Hybrid of Union and Co-op Federation

The Self-Employed Women's Association in India is an example of how unionized cooperatives can accomplish goals that traditional unions or co-ops by themselves cannot. In India, the informal sector makes up roughly 94 percent of the economy. Mirai Chatterjee, director of SEWA's Social Security unit, told me that relying on "the union approach is not going to get us anywhere when it comes to informal work." SEWA's unionized cooperative proved agile enough to accommodate the needs of informal workers, and Chatterjee believes the model could also rise to the challenges of the gig economy.

The SEWA case illustrates how a union cooperative can scale up to provide social amenities that are generally supplied by conventional unions. A nationwide trade union for 1.5 million unorganized female workers, SEWA is also a federation of 106 cooperatives with 300,000 female members.[35]

As in the United States, Chatterjee believes, in India cooperatives offer new pathways for the labor movement to help workers and expand membership. "Unions can help create collective enterprises to provide [people] with livelihoods," she said. The experience of SEWA proves that unions and co-ops are stronger together than apart. As an example of this, Chatterjee described an organization of tobacco (*bidi*) workers who hesitated to unionize for fear of losing their jobs. The SEWA union provided the tobacco workers with childcare through the cooperative, at once gaining their trust and giving them a sense of security.

This was symbiosis in action: the co-op offers social services that bring in new union members, who in turn strengthen the union's hand in agitating for policies that help workers and further enable co-ops to multiply and flourish. Cooperatives can also support unions with trade- and sector-specific training, and by setting standards across sectors.

When thinking about the roles of unions and co-ops, many people continue to use a dichotomy that is outdated and counter-productive, Chatterjee told me. "Historically, people associate unions with struggle and cooperatives with development," she said. "But this isn't always true." She continued:

> Unions and cooperatives can mutually strengthen each other; the union promotes cooperatives by organizing and building their unity first and foremost, thereby enabling their livelihood. Co-ops can bring in new members by providing livelihoods and services to unorganized workers who are not yet SEWA members. In some parts of India, different collective forms based on cooperative principles must be used [because] co-ops are not an easy option. [In such cases], unions can help with cooperative advocacy by removing taxes and developing enabling policies. They can also help to provide large markets for workers' products and services.[36]

Still, Chatterjee concedes that the potential for tension between unions and co-ops is always present to some degree. "If coop service is inadequate or unavailable," she told me, "union organizers [can] become agitated and claim that it has an impact on their membership drives because members are dissatisfied. For example, members [sometimes] become dissatisfied when 10 percent of their applications for life insurance are rejected."

On balance, synergy outweighs conflict. When a cooperative is the first to organize and register in a particular sector, Chatterjee said, a union can step in and use its influence to insist that these cooperatives are providing a form of livelihood. Once the cooperatives in that sector are established, unions can offer them the advantage of larger membership, which in turn helps create worker trusts and provides social benefits that only large organizations can offer. Chatterjee noted that many SEWA members, depending on their political leanings, identify more with the union than with its federation of cooperatives.

SEWA is notable for its constant experimentation with new forms of organizing. For example, the union is not wedded to the strategy of incorporating cooperatives, which are deeply unpopular in many parts of India, associated as they are with corruption and elite or political capture. "We are interested in new ways of organizing based on cooperative principles," Chatterjee told me. SEWA seeks to build community-based organizations for working-class people, rooted in mutuality, solidarity, ownership, and democratic governance.

Toward this end, SEWA is more interested in achieving good outcomes for workers than in ideologically promoting one form of labor organization over the other. "When we responded to women's needs and went to the mainstream banks, they would not offer services to poor women," Chatterjee recalled. "So, we had to invent our own. We chose the cooperative form of organization for SEWA Bank because it fits well with the union—it's also a workers' organization—democratic and run by an elected board of workers."

SEWA's co-op-union hybrid approach, not comfortably fitting into the category of either a cooperative or a union, has positioned it as an intriguing and innovative model for businesses, leveraging the strengths and advantages of both models. It is a kind of fusion that takes the best from both worlds. SEWA is a "fish out of water in the trade union movement, and a fish out of water within the cooperative movement," said Chatterjee. But this is a net positive. Increasing income inequality has created "a desperate need for livelihood and social protections, [and] partnerships between unions and cooperative organizations become critical," she said. "More dialogue between the trade union and the co-op movement is needed. Groups like the International Labor Organization and the Open Society Foundations facilitate these conversations."[37] In the United States, organizations such as the Service Employees International Union (SEIU), the School of Management and Labor Relations at Rutgers University, and and 1worker1vote (an organization that advocates for workplace democracy) are well positioned to facilitate dialogue between co-ops and unions.

SEWA's trade union and its cooperatives work well together because, in the end, both are aligned with SEWA's Gandhian mission to not only challenge injustice, but also construct alternative institutions *and* values—to do what Gandhi called *rachnaatmak kaam*, or "constructive work."

Associational Power in the Digital Age

How can we introduce Gandhi's twin model of "constructive work" into the digital economy? In his opening remarks to the 2017 platform co-op conference at the New School in New York City, Professor Joseph Blasi began by describing his vision for the future of the cooperative movement. "If I close my eyes and dream of a perfect future," he said, "I see unionized worker cooperatives."[38] Blasi is one of the leading experts on employee ownership in the US. When he says that unionized worker cooperatives are the key to an ideal future, it's worth paying attention.

There is some potential for realizing Blasi's dream. Trade unions have struggled to organize the digital economy, leaving gig workers vulnerable on major marketplaces like Upwork and Freelancer. However, the potential for a solution exists, for example, in union-cooperative digital labor markets that prioritize fair treatment and safety for workers and clients. Such markets could become the largest online labor markets in highly unionized countries like the Netherlands. Will unions rise to the challenge of reconnecting with their historical roots and actively participate in the development of cooperatively managed digital labor markets?

Examples also abound in other sectors in countries with less-developed labor movements. In Uganda, the Kampala Metropolitan Boda Boda Entrepreneurs Cooperative and the Airport Taxi Drivers' Cooperative have teamed up with the Amalgamated Transport and General Workers' Union to develop their own app. This unionized platform co-op aims to compete with Uber and improve wages and working conditions while fighting for other sociopolitical demands.[39] Another example, though it isn't officially a platform co-op yet, is the UK's Drive, Cardiff Taxi Co-operative, created in 2019 by the GMB union following discussions about union responses to the gig economy and steps for ensuring a decent wage.[40]

Digital platforms serve multiple purposes in the context of unionized co-ops. They can help members understand and protect their labor rights, organizing and voting through governance platforms like Loomio and Liquid Democracy, and collecting data to empower members and lobby policymakers. These tools allow dispersed workers to deliberate and vote on issues, giving them a greater say in how their work is conducted.

It is not difficult to imagine scenarios in which these tools benefit even remote rural populations. Consider the Adivasi people of India, who live in remote, difficult-to-reach mountain regions. Through platforms, they might be supplied with educational materials, a traditional union service, which would help close the literacy gap. Adivasi women who are also SEWA members are positioned to help the union move into these regions with other services, from the financial to the political.

Although unions and cooperatives are founded on the principles of collective action, they currently bring distinct sets of resources to the table. Unions offer physical infrastructure like meeting rooms, market research, lobbying power, and seed capital through credit unions. Platform co-ops, on the other hand, offer novel ways to organize self-employed gig workers and overcome anti-union laws.

This need for partnership was highlighted at the 2018 Global Labor Conference in São Paulo. From the podium, delegates from the International Transport Workers' Federation issued an impassioned call for making employee ownership the foundation for a new vision for trade unionism. The proposal was met with considerable applause from thousands of delegates eager to end the disorientation and drift that have defined the global union movement since at least the 1980s. They understand that the collapse of postwar social partnership arrangements demands new models for workers' movements in rich and poor nations alike. A growing number are also coming around to the view that the success or failure of these models cannot be determined by traditional union organizing tools and tactics. They will require excavating the shared roots of the original "friendly societies," unions, and cooperatives, and understanding how their common origins in the industrial capitalism of the nineteenth century point toward a synergetic destiny in the digital economy of the twenty-first.

6

The Coming Data Democracy

To understand the role data plays in the platform co-op vision of economic democracy, we travel to the remote beaches of Bahía de Kino, on the Pacific coast of Mexico. We arrive at dawn. Here, under the first light of day, we see men appearing with small fiberglass boats, nets, poles, and buckets, preparing to ply a trade that predates modern technology by millennia.

Our subject, let's call him Rodrigo, is a fictitious but representative fisher. Fifty years old, he inherited a small fishing business from his father, dislikes cellphones and social media, yet has ambitions to grow his operation and is beginning to recognize the importance of technology and innovation. Unlike many of his competitors, Rodrigo descends from a long line of fishermen that understood, by necessity, the importance of conserving the ocean's resources for the next generation. This is why he fishes with a line rather than a net.

Mexico's thriving fishery cooperative movement—comprising 10,217 fishers at the time of writing—will help Rodrigo to grow his operation while spreading his sustainable practices across the one-boat businesses of Bahía de Kino.[1] A fishing platform co-op is being developed that connects numerous smaller fisher co-ops to a larger data co-op that serves as a federation for selective data sharing. It allows fishers to harness data to track the monthly catches of all boats, for example, and then inform the public about the daily catch. In the spirit of peer-to-peer information sharing, fishers might even post "solutions" to issues they've overcome: how to repair fishing gear, how to develop community no-take zones, and how to adapt to climate change and shifting marine ecosystems.

Women, too, contribute to the fishery system. Let us imagine Rodrigo's wife, Maria, and their pregnant daughter work in the family business. From the shore and the family's small home office Maria could analyze the data on how the fishery is performing: Is it healthy? How many of a given species are there? What if locals were to stop fishing in a specific area to allow regeneration? She and her daughter could, in time, develop the information needed to preserve the fishery that is the economic lifeblood of the community.

But Maria begins this process with an understandable wariness: in the past, many researchers (from larger fishing operations, private companies, and the government) have offered to "empower" the local fishers, only to vanish with the information they collected from them. In essence, fishers like Rodrigo are required to collect data by law—at risk of losing their fishing licenses—but have not benefited from this collection. In a cooperative digital economy, data co-ops linked to platform co-ops can generate the network effect needed for monetization—and thus ensure that locals benefit directly from their own data. Later, I'll explain in more detail how data analytics and aggregated data help these workers.

Like fisheries across Latin America, Mexico's more than 10,000 small fishing operations were hit hard by the COVID-19 pandemic. Lacking adequate health care, the small businesses—each employing three or four fishers, on average—carried on under enormous economic pressures, with a stalled global economy making it difficult to pay boat and housing mortgages.[2] These pressures were compounded by the depletion of fish stocks, caused by climate change and by overfishing using industrial-scale trawling. The pandemic has only highlighted the need for innovation if the industry is to be made sustainable for future generations. The benefits of transitioning to the digital age, where technology can be deployed to boost revenue while also safeguarding fish stocks, are well understood by many fishers.

Data cooperatives are conceived as a sub-type of platform cooperative, one that connects individuals to one another while providing services. In one scenario, data cooperatives are created to manage platform co-ops' stakeholder data and to create value for their members, possibly with the help of a data pool or trust. Data cooperatives can function as control panels that allow their members to navigate and steer the collection and utilization of data. They are digital cooperatives owned and controlled by members with a shared interest in the use and management of data, who govern themselves through a decentralized protocol that is operated or run through software. The cooperative may use its data for a variety of purposes, such as conducting research, providing services to members, or generating revenue through the sale of data products or services.

Let's briefly return to Bahía de Kino. Consider PescaData, a data and platform cooperative developed by Comunidad y Biodiversidad (COBI) that by the end of 2021 had been used by more than 1,000 people in twelve Latin American and Caribbean countries, and that maintains a directory of 6,040 vessels and 5,614 cooperatives.[3] For years, fishers have been required by Mexico's federal government to record their daily catch data, but until the creation of the bilingual PescaData app—free to download and use—they had no control over how that data was used. According to Stuart Fulton of COBI, the fishers understand that they need "to adapt to climate change and economic changes much more quickly," and one part of this "is getting the data into their own hands," so that they can manage it themselves.[4]

The PescaData app helps with that by tracking each fishing trip's time, target species, catch volume and weight, expenses, product pricing, individual and collective income, weather conditions, and capture sites. The app also helps them rethink what this data capture could mean for them. Some are even exploring adoption of the blockchain, an appealing angle for grant-makers, who despite the technology's association with cryptocurrency and several high-profile scams continue to value its legitimate potential.

According to one fisherman from the Gulf of California, the app allows fishers to "select the data you want to share and who you are going to share [it] with. It is not just saying 'Oh, well, I am going to give away all the data from my cooperative.' You select what you want to offer."[5]

The app connects fishers with one another and with fishery organizations while also helping them market their product, services, and insights to private industry and researchers—and, if they choose, the data directly. Importantly, COBI understands that human infrastructure must exist alongside digital infrastructure. "There is an opportunity that's been missed for fishers to come together and raise their voice," said the Baja fisher.[6]

Connected through the app, fishing businesses can better organize collectively and strengthen their position vis-à-vis local authorities when it comes to influencing data-driven policies affecting the industry. A growing number of local and foreign actors recognize PescaData's ability to facilitate collective problem-solving and sectorial organizing among a geographically distributed community. Along with support from the local and federal governments in Mexico, COBI is collaborating with Stanford University to document how small-scale fisheries adapt to change.

Ines Lopez, change catalyzer at COBI, notes, "There has to be an equitable return of the benefits that have been produced."[7]

By improving fishery data, the app incentivizes the same risk-benefit mitigation strategies that we have seen with agricultural cooperatives. One echo between land and sea is the Grower's Information Services Cooperative (GISC), a growers' data co-op that aggregates anonymous data in order to cross-check weather predictions, to help farmers with business decisions and marketing.[8] Although focusing solely on monetizing the data may not yield significant results for PescaData given the limited amount of data generated by the fishers, there are other unexplored avenues through which the data can still improve the lives of the fishers. There are also similarities between COBI and Shyro, the health-data cooperative,[9] and a range of others, from Driver's Seat and CoMetrics to the worker co-op–adjacent dOrg.tech.[10] Each example offers a glimpse of a future data economy that is more just, equitable and democratic.

Data co-ops offer a business model applicable across the full range of economic activity, from restructuring Mexico's small-scale fishing industry to building a more decentralized internet. Indeed, there is a growing consensus among legal scholars, social scientists, and technologists that the co-op model presents a workable solution for the governance of data. It would end the current practice of extreme data extraction—what economists now consider acceptable "financialization"— in a way that honors the wishes and dignity of individuals and communities, who should be sovereign over their data.

In this debate, crucial questions are raised: How can data be liberated from private interests and restructured to allow its creators to access, control, and reuse it for the benefit of communities and the general public? Who should hold the keys to the data library? Whose interests are supported by digital infrastructure?

What kinds of data should digital platforms collect? How will it be analyzed and sold? Where will the new boundaries around informed consent be drawn? And who will be responsible for drawing them?

These questions represent the crux of the matter. If we do not begin to explore questions around datafication and consent with rigor, our agency and autonomy become further compromised by the dominance of a few corporations. Luckily, there are plenty of guideposts to shape and drive the discussion and debate, some of them suggestive and emergent, others already in full and ambitious use.

Explorations in the World of Nascent Data Co-ops

Any number of buzzy phrases can be thrown around to capture the zeitgeist of the governance revolution: data stewardship, bottom-up data dignity, data ownership, data altruism, data trusts, data coalitions, data collaboratories, data unions, data sovereignty, and user dignity, to name just a few. All express aspects of the project to devolve data to the people, a project that's led some researchers to liken data cooperatives to earlier forms of democratized power, such as trusts and unions. *Often it is not even clear what "data" are in fact referred to—medical data, social media data, genetic data, financial data, search data, location data?* Is the discussion about personal data alone or also business and public data? A term that has drawn considerable interest is "data trust."

Scholars and activists have defined data trusts as fiduciary trusts used to govern and maintain shared resources such as public lands, pension funds, and, increasingly, data. Data trusts can serve as a valuable tool in the arsenal of the solidarity economy, functioning as legal frameworks that govern and safeguard individuals' data. Trustees, entrusted with fiduciary duties, make decisions regarding data usage on behalf of the individuals involved, ensuring their interests are protected and maintained. Trusts in general are almost 1,000 years old, dating back to the Norman invasion of England—and they have been used to manage resources ever since. Like powers of attorney, data trusts are flexible and de facto global in reach, meaning that they can be written in ways that create legally accountable governance structures. It's helpful to think about a data trust as a container— one that can hold assets, define governance, and manage liabilities. When used for governance, data trusts can steward, maintain, and manage how data is used and shared—from who is allowed access to it, and under what terms, to who gets to define the terms, and how. They can involve a number of approaches to solving a range of problems, creating different structures to experiment with governance models and solutions in an agile way."[11]

Data trusts, when properly understood, serve as a link between service-related data, obtained with consent by data cooperatives, and the wider public. Data trusts could be used to redirect data toward social purposes or financial benefit. A data trust might be established to allow businesses to share data about energy consumption, potentially increasing energy efficiency. Another possibility is to use data about health and social care services to improve care quality and efficiency. "The collective setting of terms by the Trust is a way for data subjects to pool their rights to acquire a 'voice,'" writes the British legal scholar Sylvie Delacroix.[12] This represents an extension into the digital age of the role historically played by "land societies" that gave political voice to marginal groups.[13]

You do not have to look far to find examples of data cooperatives engaged in this rewiring. The health sector alone has three notable data co-ops pushing the bleeding edge of a new digital economy. As discussed, the oldest of these, MIDATA, was launched in September 2015 as a "health data cooperative" and enables citizens to establish and own national or regional not-for-profit

MIDATA cooperatives. These, in turn, enable their cooperative owners to securely store, manage, and control access to their personal data.

MIDATA co-ops act as the fiduciaries for their members' data and provide platforms on which user-members can securely store copies of their medical records, genomes, and mobile health data. Members might decide, for example, to give their physicians access to all personal data through the platform. In contrast, a not-for-profit cancer research institute could be given access only to medical and dietary information. Members could deny access to a for-profit drug company. Members' revenues from the sale of data are donated to public research.

Another next-generation co-op in the health-care industry is Savvy Cooperative, an online marketplace where health-related companies and innovators connect directly with diverse patients and consumers to obtain patient insights for clinical, user experience, and market research. With its thirty-three staff members, the co-op aims to solve a riddle: How is it that an industry focused on improving the lives of patients can produce so many products and services that not only fail to improve anything but sometimes makes things worse? The founders of Savvy believe the answer is simple: Patient ideas and insights are sidelined, when they should be essential in the provision of health care.

At the heart of the Savvy Cooperative—self-described on its website as the "Match.com of patient insights," a slightly offbeat analogy, perhaps—is a desire to bridge the communications gap that currently separates medical companies and innovators from patients and caregivers. With its more than 500 members, Savvy is more than a gig economy marketplace for patient insights—it is the first and only patient-owned platform. Controversially for some, it is also the first platform co-op to seek and receive venture capital funding. "Mutual venture funding" is a type of venture capital funding that cooperatives have historically used to invest in the creation of new cooperatives; however, this is different from the risk capital that emanates from Silicon Valley.[14]

Working to increase understanding of the need for data co-ops in the health sector and beyond is the data co-op polypoly. Launched in 2020, polypoly produced a tool that visualizes data flows in users' computers. Recognizing that education is vital for the future growth of data cooperatives, the founders have effectively introduced visual material to explain their approach, thereby stirring the debate on "data ownership." None of the personal data tracked by the co-op leaves the user's device, whether mobile phone, computer, or web-enabled toaster. Indeed, one polypoly project, polyPod, offers "a container hosting an individual's personal data predicated on the GDPR [that] provides infrastructure for services working with that data."[15]

This is aligned with the co-op's stance that all personal data belong to the user, not to large private data monopolies. That said, the polypoly model does not stop users from selling their data for individual profit if they so wish. Indeed, polypoly prides itself on enabling "citizens to participate for the first time in the profits that have been generated using their personal data."[16] The advancement of the project is an early test of the extent to which individual data can be monetized with current technology. Members of the polypoly Cooperative can help shape or control polypoly and the polyPod in addition to benefiting financially from it.

Whether the project succeeds in every aspect or not, users of polypoly tools are more likely to appreciate the services offered by data-respectful platform co-ops of all kinds. The Driver's Seat app, for example, helps ride-share and delivery drivers harvest and control their own data, which carries a host of benefits, enabling them to maximize efficiency, keep independent records of their earnings, and decouple their GPS tracking and messaging capabilities from centralized actors. Members of Driver's Seat

Cooperative elect and serve on the co-op board and are eligible to share the platform's profits.

Data cooperatives are emerging across sectors and industries to ensure that data is collected and democratically controlled for the benefit of members. While the prospect of financializing collected data may not be entirely realistic due to a lack of network effect, similar to what we saw with PescaData, the search is on for ways of putting those data to meaningful use, and Driver's Seat Cooperative serves as a good example of that. Understanding data as shared resources not only enables the enhancement of worker well-being but also transforms data into effective tools for developing and upholding open- and shared-data standards and legal regimes. The Data Governance Act of the EU specifically mentions the possibility of developing data cooperatives and offers a basic legal foundation for it.[17]

Community Data Renaissance: The Italian Co-op Approach

To bridge the gap between those who create data and those with stakes and a say in its use: that is the challenge of the twenty-first-century data economy.

The current data economy is one of vast, unsustainable, and appalling power asymmetries, defined by centralization, surveillance, and misuse. Apps and devices are designed to leverage value from the daily activities of their users, including information about where we live, our health, our finances, our sexual preferences, our religious beliefs, and our political affiliations. This information is gathered when we browse the internet, make purchases, travel around cities, or use social media.

As seen in the market capitalization of data-driven corporate platforms and technological firms, today data is critical to accumulating and wielding economic and political power. Amazon, Apple, Microsoft, Meta, Alphabet, Salesforce, Netflix, Uber, Twitter,

Intuit, and Paypal have the highest market capitalizations in the United States. SAP, Takeaway, Spotify, and Delivery Hero have some of the highest in Europe. In China, there are Alibaba, Tencent, and Mei, and in the Asia-Pacific region more broadly, Samsung. In Africa there is Prosus and Naspers, and in Latin America, Mercado Libre.

This power is now held in silos by just a few government and private institutions, whose control over and processing of data generates a network effect: the more data points collected, the more value created for the data set as a whole and the actor in control of the data. There is a growing consensus that a new regime of data governance is needed based on more distributed decision-making.

This transition must rest on the understanding that data generation is a form of unpaid, invisible, collective labor. This is not a new insight; it was spotlighted in the 1970s in the ideas of the Italian Workerists, and in particular, in Mario Tronti's concept of the "society-factory" or "social factory."[18] Also relevant is Dallas Smythe's foundational argument that audiences should be viewed as the primary product created by broadcasters and advertising outlets. He claimed that the media industry, driven by the imperative to generate advertising revenues, became focused on mass production and mass consumption. Theorists such as Michael Hardt and Antonio Negri, Yann Moulier Boutang, Sut Jhally, and Christian Fuchs explained that social participation and value extraction are inextricably linked. As a result, how media content is created and distributed has changed dramatically.

Translating Smythe and Tronti for today's world, the data generated from our digital activities and social relations generate financial value comparable to industrial-age economic production, with the digital attention economy serving as a factory without walls, with the product—each of us—contributing to a massive opaque, constant, and often unwitting value capture by the major tech companies.[19]

It's no surprise, then, that some internet-dominating companies built their power through the collection and analysis of data. However, data is often mistakenly conceived of as an individual asset. On the contrary, by itself personal data has minimal monetary value. As scholars Alex Pentland and Thomas Hardjono contend, "People often think of monetizing personal data, but the reality is that while there is a great deal of value in aggregate data for specific purposes, there is no market mechanism for data exchange, and so personal data does not have very much value on an individual basis."[20] Data sets of entire demographics, on the other hand, are extremely valuable for their use in predictive analytics. This is why AI-based technology developed in the R&D labs of large tech companies focus on studying "aggregated data sets," only later "applying these insights back to [individual] people."[21] They understand that the true economic value of data derives from the aggregation of information generated by large groups.

"We can think of data aggregation as the assembly of a new final product—an advertising base, a predictive model—where only industrial-scale operations have the ability to produce a product for which a market exists," notes one group of scholars and practitioners.[22] PescaData is a good example of this. Data generated by one fishing cooperative or fisher is insignificant to large tech companies, but data from all of the fishers along Mexico's Pacific Coast can lead to insights of enormous commercial value.

In one of my previous books, *UberWorked and Underpaid*, I called this group extraction of data "crowd fleecing." Data democracy can end this practice by treating data as a *collective economic resource*. We should perceive our online searches and purchases not merely as private actions but rather as collective endeavors.

Cooperatives and Data Democracy

There is a long tradition of cooperatives addressing social problems at scale, especially when supported by regulation. In the early 1930s, Franklin Roosevelt's administration addressed the Great Depression in part by taking aim at the overconcentration of energy production in large cities. Most of the generators at the time were located in urban areas, many of them paid for by companies that had no interest in extending electricity to rural customers—a situation similar to today's urban-rural split in the distribution of broadband internet.

The Rural Electrification Administration (REA), as part of the New Deal, granted loans to electric cooperatives to construct power lines and electric generators to serve rural areas. With the help of REA, electric cooperatives increased the percentage of rural households with electricity from 13 percent in 1929 to 94 percent in 1944.[23] In a modern-day echo of this history, some US electricity co-ops are thinking of ways to create e-car charging stations for underserved areas. They certainly have the reach to make an immediate impact: electric cooperatives provide power to 42 million people in households, businesses, farms, and schools across more than half of the nation's territory. Members of the Mobility Factory SCE platform cooperative in the EU include a renewable energy cooperative and electric car-sharing cooperatives, some of which have funded such charging stations.

The example of the REA shows that cooperatives can serve the public good at scale. It remains an inspiring demonstration of how regulation might address the very different challenge posed by a highly concentrated data economy. Franklin D. Roosevelt created a community asset in an area where private companies had no incentive to solve a problem. There are plenty of places where today's governments might begin to create outposts of data democracy—for example, by allowing cooperative ownership of health data.[24] The potential for data standards leadership lies within the International Labour Organization (ILO), the specialized agency of the United Nations that focuses on promoting social justice and decent work.

Data Rights as Labor Rights

A useful distinction should be made here between data ownership and data stewardship. The former is currently unrealistic; the latter—implying control and access—can be achieved today in myriad ways. But whatever forms this reclamation takes, it will require public and cooperative digital infrastructure. There is only so much local actors can do. A data co-op cannot replace data warehouses and will require public cloud services to compete with Google's cloud and Amazon Web Services.

We must also ensure that this information is in the hands of the appropriate individuals, allowing decision-makers access to it while also enabling citizens to better monitor and hold the decision-makers accountable. Transparency of the entire data system is a crucial component of this. As the discussion about data ownership broadens and deepens, practitioners, theorists, and the public will expand our understanding of how our data is used and by whom. Indeed, merely raising the question of "data ownership"—introducing it to the political lexicon—has important educational effects.

The discussion of data democracy must not be left to elite legal scholars and policymakers who believe they know what's best for the public. This process requires active leadership by the communities and co-ops driving innovation in a participatory manner. A successful transformation should be powered by their vision and imagination, grounded in their experiences, and rooted in pilot projects emerging from communities determined to take control of their data to use it for the common good.

As full data democracy is achieved in stages, we can, along the way, increase the transparency of data systems and applications in important ways. A feminist or Indigenous critique of data collection, for example, might highlight how data collection targets or ignores sub-groups in the wider population. The goal, however, is an uprising led by communities demanding education, accountability, and the fundamental rights to access, stewardship, and control of digital infrastructure, including cooperative hybrid infrastructure and every bit (and byte) of their data. At the 2022 PCC conference in Rio, Anita Gurumurthy, an Indian feminist researcher and digital rights activist, emphatically proclaimed the need to develop a concept of data rights as labor rights, emphasizing that they are the new worker rights.

Once again, the sharing of private health data presents itself as a useful starting point for public education. So, too, do ride-hailing taxi apps. The city of Barcelona has claimed, for example, that the data that e-scooters or Uber taxis create when crisscrossing the city belongs not to the companies but to the municipality. While the Spanish government may not adopt Barcelona's approach to data sovereignty and possesses the authority to override it (given the limited power of cities), the act of challenging gig economy platforms such as Uber and Deliveroo, and proposing an alternative model, carries symbolic significance beyond the borders of Spain.

At the time of this writing, the legal discussion about data ownership is limited. Significantly, the EU has created a comprehensive data regulation regime called the General Data Protection Regulation (GDPR). The law regulates data privacy and protection in the European Union—European Economic Area in two directions: streamlining the regulatory environment for multinational corporations, and giving individuals increased control over their personal data. Any business that processes the personal data of EU residents is required to adhere to the GDPR's requirements.

One of the rights granted to "data subjects" by the GDPR is the ability to exercise data portability. This approach lets internet users request that any data they contributed to a specific service be put in a machine-readable format so that it can be transferred to a new service provider if desired. Such data portability addresses the network effects that favor large tech companies, making it easier for users of a social media service, for example, to leave that platform for a competitor. The European Digital Services Act and the Digital Markets Act are also relevant when it comes to user rights and protection.[25]

The EU policy encounters significant challenges in its implementation, however, as the rapid development of new technologies outpaces the measured stride of democracy, posing hurdles for policymakers striving to keep up.

This global debate is unfolding in academic and civic circles. In New Zealand, for example, a growing movement for Māori data sovereignty advocates for the recognition of Māori rights and interests in data, along with the ethical use of data to enhance the well-being of Māori people, language and culture.[26] The Māori initiative has echoes in efforts by Indigenous groups in Australia and the United States. While not technically a digital initiative, it was formed in a similar spirit, embodying the slogan adopted by the movement of people with disabilities: "Nothing about us without us."[27]

Participation Rules, Technology Supports

Project Cybersyn, an ambitious endeavor conceived in 1971 under the leadership of Chilean president Salvador Allende, aimed to explore an alternative economic planning system within a socialist framework. It brought together a team of engineers and scientists who worked diligently on this short-lived initiative. Cybersyn is an example of a socialist state's embrace of participatory data governance. Conceived as a distributed decision-support system to aid in the management of the national economy, the project consisted of four modules: an economic simulator, a computer network linking factories to one another and the central government, telex machines for updating data sets, and an operations room where ministries could monitor economic indicators in real time. Although the project was not completed during Allende's truncated term in office, it was notable for its use of pioneering cybernetic ideas.

The legacy of Project Cybersyn extends to inspiring the development of modern-day data governance mechanisms at both local and global scales.[28] Among the intellectual descendants of Cybersyn, a nonprofit foundation has developed Decidim, an open-source platform for participatory democracy. The software is designed to facilitate citizen participation in the democratic process, and has been used by cities and organizations such as the Barcelona City Council and the Government of Catalonia. Developed as part of En Comú Podem's initiatives to engage citizens in the city's public affairs, Decidim serves not only municipal governance, but also any purpose or group that encourages collaboration. It was used to create strategic planning for the city of Barcelona in 2016–17, a process that involved more than 80 citizen meetings and 8,000 citizen recommendations. Decidim has since grown into its own online democratic community, with the goal of cultivating democratic culture. The platform allows residents to get together and have their opinions heard on the decisions that affect their lives. In this way, it actively creates a more participatory and transparent form of government. Notably, the platform's source code is available to all on GitHub.

In the dynamic realm of democracy, the liberal representative model stands strong, while co-ops embrace diverse democratic approaches such as participatory and deliberative models. Kleros, a French dispute-resolution platform, is among the digital co-ops pushing the boundaries of governance. It pioneers innovative governance approaches by modernizing the ancient Greek method of sortition, using small virtual juries of users to analyze disputes and deliver rulings. Loomio, another digital offshoot of Cybersyn, is a globally utilized digital tool that facilitates thoughtful and productive deliberation, and enables group decision-making.[29]

Then there is quadratic voting, a distinctive method that offers an alternative to binary voting systems. Unlike tools or platforms such as Loomio or Kleros, quadratic voting is a voting mechanism that allows individuals to express preferences on a scale from 1 to 10. Recognizing the value of quadratic voting in capturing diverse degrees of preference and importance, co-ops embrace this nuanced approach to enhance democratic processes and achieve fairer outcomes, alongside other tools and platforms. However, these examples are only one piece of the user governance puzzle; robust dispute-resolution processes and clear community rules are also required to guarantee that everyone feels heard and decisions are made in good faith.

Beyond governance platforms and voting mechanisms, the Italian approach to community cooperatives presents an inspiring model deeply rooted in the concept of a multipurpose or community cooperative. These cooperatives focus on producing goods or services that benefit the broader community, transcending the boundaries of their own membership. Interest in community cooperatives has grown greatly since the 2000s, just as they have expanded into a variety of sectors, including energy and rural regeneration.[30] To push back against the depopulation of Italian townships, there has been a trend toward revitalization through promoting tourism and social development, and these co-ops play a role in that process.

Take the example of Genoa Il Cesto cooperative, located in the Italian port city of Genoa. This community cooperative collects and distributes surplus food, sells organic and fair trade products, and organizes cultural and educational events, including music festivals. Originally established to support children in need, the cooperative has since expanded to include not only its members but also volunteers and community members who work together to address the needs of marginalized groups such as abused women, immigrants, and the homeless. Despite being a small cooperative, the Genoa Il Cesto has seen growth since 2015, with membership increasing from just four to forty members.

The community cooperative approach is particularly powerful in the smaller, rural Italian townships, where co-op members may have diverse responsibilities, ranging from managing a small hotel and restaurant to running the post office, and even looking after sheep. Community cooperatives, when applied as a model to different contexts and geographies, have the potential to make a contribution to the public-minded capture and use of data.

Data Commons: A Rising Tide Lifts All Boats

While companies treat data as a commodity to trade, a data commons recognizes data as a shared collective resource that belongs to all. Such data commons are anchored in the sixth cooperative principle, which states that cooperatives should support one another. Members of a cooperative data commons would be able to pool their data resources and knowledge to tackle common challenges.

Shared data standards and interoperability will be key. Establishing a cooperative data commons demands a shared understanding and agreed-upon protocols, underscoring the significance of a global steward for this work. In this regard, the International Cooperative Alliance is a natural choice to take on an active role as facilitator of this effort. The lack of shared protocols mirrors the situation faced by the pioneers of the internet in the early 1970s, such as Vint Cerf, who went from one organization to the next appealing to them to use the free TCP/IP protocol. Data portability is another consideration. While federated social networks like Diaspora, GNU Social, Mastodon, or Friendica have been in existence for some time, they have faced limitations as most people's rich social links—their infamous "social graph"—are locked within dominant platforms.[31]

Imagine the transformative potential of seamlessly exporting not only your Meta connections but your entire activity history to rival social networks owned and controlled by a federation of user-run cooperatives. This paradigm shift challenges the dominance of platforms that heavily rely on the network effect instead of innovation. To realize this vision, regulatory intervention is crucial for dismantling the barriers that confine our social graph and enabling data portability.

The current economy is built on this lock-in approach, as seen in open data rules requiring banks to use the same machine-readable standardized data through open APIs. Use of such standardized open data will be necessary to generate innovation in the co-op sector. In a 2022 study, COBI's Stuart Fulton argued that lack of interoperability is the "principal impediment" to the creation of the data commons. Until now, he writes, digital technologies "have not been designed to interoperate, meaning that the value we collect, curate, and create [cannot] be shared, discovered, adopted, and adapted with ease."[32]

The most cost-effective and time-efficient way to make knowledge more accessible and shareable is through a common digital infrastructure. This requires the formal design and engineering of previously unconnected products across organizational boundaries, in compliance with current privacy standards.

One potential scenario for a cooperative data commons is exemplified by Parana Uniti, a network comprising twenty-one cooperatives located in the state of Paraná, Brazil. This cooperative network made the decision to establish UniTI, the first central information technology cooperative, with the objective of reducing software costs and facilitating data sharing among cooperatives. This initiative represents a low-hanging fruit that can bring significant benefits to cooperatives.

The vision of Parana Uniti is also shared by Nathan Schneider. "I envision clusters of small, reliable cloud cooperatives whose members have shared affinity," he writes. "They self-finance their maintenance costs while participating in the development of the open-source software they rely on. As a result, we see a mass exodus of users from the one-size-fits-all surveillance platforms [and] an explosion of open-source software with awesome user interfaces because the development is user-funded."[33] As interest in a cooperative data commons grows, we must remain vigilant against potential "solidarity impostors." Already there are signs that defenders of the status quo may deploy fake cooperatives that manipulate the cooperative spirit. Several Web3 projects, despite being venture capital–funded, claim to have a cooperative approach yet lack the core aspects of a genuine cooperative. Co-op Commerce, for instance, has garnered $5.8 million in venture capital funding, defying the notion that cooperatives do not sell such equity.[34]

It is indeed a delicate balancing act to uphold cooperative principles without adopting the role of a co-op watchdog that stifles emerging experiments. Nurturing and supporting these experiments are essential, as is discerning genuine cooperative endeavors from instances of "co-op washing," where the appearance of cooperation masks ulterior motives or a lack of true commitment to cooperative principles. Stepping away from centralized cloud services and embracing alternative options like Holochain is a step toward a data commons, as these options provide support for genuine cooperative initiatives. This ambitious project aims to create an "alternative to the dominant centralized systems of the Internet, protecting our ability to make our own choices, and giving trustworthy information we can act on."[35]

Holochain exists on an encrypted peer-to-peer network that allows participants to use their own devices to create identities and maintain ownership of their data. It is impossible to control, shut down, or co-opt data on Holochain. Furthermore, users no longer have to pay for cloud hosting. Holochain has already produced workable health-care and social media apps, as well as a software protocol integrated in devices that produce, consume or store electricity.[36] It has done this using the hype of the blockchain without building an actual distributed ledger.

The example of Holochain's application of free and open-source software could help some platform cooperatives shift away from proprietary data and coding models. At the same time, it's important to understand that one size does not fit all, and there is a difference between *source-available* and *open source*. Some co-ops may have good reasons to forgo an open-source approach and instead protect code through a peer-production or Creative Commons Plus license. This would make their code available to other cooperatives but not to all entities that might seek to exploit it.

Credit Unions as the Beachheads of Data Democracy?

The computer scientist Alex "Sandy" Pentland has proposed that American credit unions are perfectly situated to become beachheads of data democracy, as well as models for data co-ops more generally. With their millions of members, he argues, "the opportunity for community organizations to leverage community-owned data is huge."[37] Pentland suggests that credit union–based data co-ops could aggregate statistics about their community for the community's benefit. "Communities need data about their economic health in order to plan their future, but the data required for neighborhood-level planning is unavailable to them," he writes. "With the development of community-owned data cooperatives this could change dramatically."[38]

Pentland's suggestion to utilize credit unions as a model for data governance aligns with my recommendation to draw inspiration from the synergy between Cybersyn and Italian community models when designing effective data governance frameworks. While credit unions have a significant presence in the US, their democratic participation has been met with mixed success, and they often struggle to maintain clear distinctions from conventional banks. Repurposing existing structures like credit unions or community cooperatives is not without challenges, yet it offers a meaningful and practical way to socialize ideas and leverage established networks.[39] It is worth considering the opinion of technologist and activist Nabil Hassein that new structures may be needed, as reforming existing structures can be challenging. In the US, for example, the often racist nature of the federal and municipal system hinders fair representation for marginalized communities.

> Liberation of Black folks and all oppressed peoples will never be achieved by inclusion in systems controlled by a capitalist elite which benefits from the perpetuation of racism and related oppressions. The struggle for liberation is not a struggle for diversity and inclusion—it is a struggle for decolonization, reparations, and self-determination.[40]

But American credit unions may be well suited for Pentland's experiment. They serve a diverse clientele, with 34 percent being minorities. Among them, the largest Black-owned credit union manages over $625 million in assets, making it a promising starting point. These examples demonstrate alternative approaches that prioritize democratic participation, community empowerment, and responsible use of data.

Data on Blockchains

No technology has been more hyped in recent years as a tool to combat data centralization than blockchains—the technological innovation underlying cryptocurrencies and the emerging iteration of the internet known as Web3. Popularly known for hosting the ownership and trading records of thousands of digital currencies, the blockchain's potential to revolutionize governance (in theory) and make data portable has led some in the cooperative movement to praise the technology for its capacity to enable greater democracy and profoundly affect the global economy.[41] Discouraged by events like the collapse of cryptocurrency and blockchain platforms FTX and Terra Luna, some argue that blockchains offer no viable use case for the left and are viewed as an unscrupulous racket promoted by a depoliticized libertarian project. I think that while it is not necessary to embrace every utopian promise surrounding distributed ledgers, it is important to acknowledge that these technologies hold the potential to contribute, in some capacity, to the development of a cooperative economy.[42]

But one need not believe every utopian promise—or conspiratorial dismissal—regarding distributed ledgers to understand that decentralized Web3 applications have the potential to advance the building of the cooperative economy. Yes, the technology is most closely associated with a market that often resembles a giant Ponzi scheme, but it is naive to overlook the quantity and quality of governance, community-building, and finance experiments occurring beyond the spotlighted frame of Bitcoin and Dogecoin.

Just as with Web 2.0, *something* always happens when people spend billions of dollars. Projects do get built, not all goes to waste. No less an authority than Tim Berners-Lee, coinventor of the World Wide Web, contends that a handful of Big Tech firms leverage our personal data to lock us into their platforms. Yet he remains skeptical of blockchain. "Ignore the Web3 stuff," he says.[43]

Even so, as a testament to the blockchain's potentially game-changing implications for the ownership and monetization of data, Berners-Lee founded Solid, a set of rules and tools for developing decentralized social applications based on the ideas of Linked Data, a model in which our data are no longer stored by the apps we use, but rather are stored and linked in a decentralized manner. Berners-Lee is currently conducting pilot projects in partnership with the BBC, the British National Health Service, and the regional government of Flanders in Belgium. His team is also at work on a data-access library to enable the building of decentralized apps, or Dapps, with the goal of bringing "radical change to the way Web applications work today, resulting in true data ownership as well as improved privacy."[44]

By embracing a broad definition for platform cooperatives, we can create space for the emergence of protocolary co-ops, which offer a decentralized alternative without a central point of control or a "kill switch," distinguishing them from the democratically centralized platforms commonly associated with platform cooperatives. Projects like Solid, the data co-op–credit union hybrid, community coops, and other initiatives form an ocean of solutions that, while they may not fully reclaim the internet, have the potential to mitigate some of the harm caused by concentration.

Decentralized Autonomous Organizations

Decentralized autonomous organizations (DAOs) have emerged as an integral technology on the democratic-data frontier. DAOs can be used in many ways, and are often overhyped, but they essentially allow for decentralized governance by operating on the rails of smart contracts coded onto a blockchain. This type of organization has numerous advantages, from increased transparency to decreased costs of coordination. DAOs are more nimble and technically (though not operationally) more resistant to corruption than traditional top-down organizations. Though still in their early stages, DAOs have already begun to attract attention for their potential to create new forms of digital ownership and to distribute that ownership in novel ways.

The first-ever DAO, known simply as the DAO, raised more than $150 million to establish a type of crowdfunded investment firm—a decentralized Kickstarter—only to fail because of a slew of legal, governance, and code vulnerability flaws. And yet this innovative new system has the potential to change the way we think about governance and community management forever.

The DAO model is not without its critics within the co-op movement. One platform co-op, DisCO, has even published a full manifesto critiquing DAOs as a cover for bad actors who do not share cooperative values or goals. However, there are ways to thwart the use of DAOs as fronts for "fake" cooperatives.

One takes a cue from the German software developer Dmytri Kleiner. In his *Telekommunist Manifesto*, Kleiner writes that "platforms must not depend on servers and admins, even when cooperatively run, but must, to the greatest degree possible, run on the computers of the platforms' users." By ensuring that computational capacity remains in members' hands, he continues, "we prevent the communication platform from becoming capital, and we prevent the users from being instrumentalized as an audience commodity."[45]

Despite the predatory nature of certain blockchain implementations, dismissing their potential to contribute to the public good would be shortsighted. The world of DAOs showcases a range of legitimate community-self-help efforts and research initiatives, such as the NYC-based Mutual Aid DAO, Work DAO, Labor DAO, and Opolis. These entities operate within legal structures that facilitate democratic governance and provide benefits to their users.

There is a deepening public recognition that the centralized ownership of data is neither democratic nor sustainable. The realization of data democracy, however, is far from guaranteed. To realize their potential, data co-ops must address and resolve a number of challenges and open questions. Chief among them is governance. Data co-ops require clear and transparent rules that delineate how data is collected and used, and how members can join and leave and take their data with them.

Democratic data collection and management will require calibrating a balance between individual privacy concerns and the interests and wishes of the larger community. Because there is no one-size-fits-all solution, it will be up to each co-op to decide when, for example, to restrict data collection in the interests of personal privacy, and when to sacrifice privacy in favor of shared goals prioritized by members. Finally, data cooperatives must remain flexible when it comes to adapting and adopting new technologies. To bring the vision of a cooperative data commons and a more decentralized internet to fruition, the cooperative movement must actively support and promote practical initiatives that align with its principles, recognizing that technology experimentation may not be feasible for individuals with immediate existential needs.

7

Letter from 2035:
A Social Vision Realized

The following letter is from the near future—twelve years after the publication of this book, to be precise. The tradition of social speculative fiction is a long one, and it is in that tradition that I hope to inspire the present through imagining what may lie ahead. This is a hopeful imagining, to be sure, but it is rooted in current trends and based on real-world actors, most of whom we have met in the preceding chapters. I was inspired as much by the French theorist André Gorz as by the classics of speculative fiction, such as Edward Bellamy's Looking Backward. *Specifically, this chapter is a response to the injunction issued by Gorz in his 1967 book,* Strategy for Labor: A Radical Proposal. *"Now more than ever," he wrote, "it is necessary to present not only an overall alternative but also those 'intermediate objectives' (mediations) which lead to it and foreshadow it in the present. A different model of consumption [and production] is of a much more real and revolutionary significance than all the abstract speeches about the billions pocketed by monopolies."[1]*

What follows is a description of how one alternative model, in synergy with others, might be put into action, not in the distant future, but soon enough to meaningfully meet the multiple emergencies of the twenty-first century. To those who would prefer to focus imaginative energy on a more distant utopia, and who would discourage satisfaction with more realistic near-term successes, I argue that there is no need to choose. Grounding ourselves pragmatically in the present does not require giving up on the long-term goal of a fully transformed society. But such a transformation can only be achieved in stages, one of which is the subject of the following.

June 2, 2035

Dear Reader,

I write you shortly after the publication of the latest World Economic Forum report, "The Future of Work: 2035–2050." This remarkable document provides detailed analysis of the accelerating global proliferation of platform cooperatives over the past decade or so, and projects forward. As of the current count, more than eighty countries have established programs and model laws to support the development of platform cooperatives, with many expressing interest in doing the same. Some of the projects highlighted in the report are catalysts for businesses run on cooperative principles, with notable activity in Berlin, Germany; Umeå, Sweden; and Trivandrum (Thiruvananthapuram), India. But Costa Rica and Peru have also emerged as regional leaders. "After Hurricane Etna and then during the height of the pandemic, the shortage of nurses hit us hard. We thought about telemedicine and platform co-ops emerged as a possibility," said Luis, a co-op leader in San José.

In the world of tech platforms, it is important to acknowledge that not all ventures are a win. In 2035, even prominent platform co-ops, particularly in domains like music streaming, have faced challenges. Amid these hurdles, however, there have also been remarkable success stories. In 2026, Fairbnb gained significant support from Italy's cooperative alliance. Two years later, the

Fairbnb Foundation enabled global communities to create their own versions of the platform using open-source software. This decentralized approach led to widespread adoption of Fairbnb beyond Italy and northern Spain, promoting fair and sustainable travel in the short-term rental market.

By 2035, digital marketplaces like Amavida Market, meaning "community" in Zulu, supported sewing co-ops in South African townships like Manenberg, and similar, sometimes hyperlocal digital marketplaces supported rural Adivasi women in Gujarat, India. Part analog, part online, Kasebkoop in Iran bridged the gap between online marketplaces and local shopkeepers. Musicians, poets, and domestic workers in Lebanon, Dhaka, and Brazil led initiatives, removing exploitative intermediaries in the arts, culture, and domestic work sectors. Inspired by unjust practices on platforms like Etsy, producers have taken matters into their own hands by establishing platform cooperatives, reclaiming ownership, and ensuring fair profits. A hybrid model emerged in 2035, combining the British platform co-op Equal Care with Italian social co-ops in territories with supportive legislation, addressing the growing need for care in an aging population. Global artificial intelligence cooperatives such as Machine Learning Guild and AI Sisters drove innovation for inclusive, fair, and transparent AI. Lastly, the remarkable expansion of the Drivers Cooperative in New York City exemplified the transformative power of collective efforts, with 20,000 members in the early 2030s providing 175,000 daily rides.

Pioneering projects initiated by the self-identified "new cooperators" have emerged within Brazil's homeless movement, the migrant movements of the late 2020s and early 2030s, and the International Union of App-Based Transport Workers, which was established last year in Tokyo during the fourth annual meeting of the Platform Transport Alliance. In this transformative era, we witness an increasing number of these "new cooperators" taking their commitment to change beyond cooperative organizations and venturing into electoral politics. From the Ministry of Culture in Columbia to the Argentine Congress, these dedicated policymakers bring with them a feminist agenda and a vision for a "wellness economy." When they talk about digital platforms, they also talk about childcare, equal representation, care work, fairly remunerating unpaid or underpaid work, and the value of joy. Women and gender-expansive "new cooperators" actively contribute in decision-making, prioritize safe digital environments, and ensure transparency, accountability, and freedom from gender bias in the development and training of AI systems. So, that makes it even more crucial that the World Economic Forum predicts that by 2045, the number of platform co-ops will double, serving over 100 million members and customers worldwide.

This year's World Economic Forum report on the future of work distinguishes itself from previous reports by emphasizing the role of cooperatives as a driving force in poverty elimination in many low- and middle-income countries, as well as a significant contributor to the United Nations' progress in meeting its Sustainable Development Goals.

The year 2035 was also a critical turning point that compelled us to confront the consequences of our past actions as catastrophic climate events unfolded before our eyes. We faced a surge in frighteningly extreme weather events, rising sea levels, related humanitarian crises, and an urgent need for economic recalibration and sustainable practices. In response, platform co-ops stand as one pillar of the solidarity economy and the pro-commons movement, offering a distinct and powerful alternative to existing organizational forms. In the early 2020s, there was a surge of interest in integrating cooperative values into DAOs and implementing cooperative governance for the purpose of building more equitable, collectively owned organizations.

Models and labels in the tech industry often go through a period
of intense hype before gradually losing popularity and transitioning into a phase of more substantial but less glamorous long-term
experimentation. This slower phase focuses on making a
meaningful impact and involves in-depth exploration and testing
of innovative approaches. It's not for the impatient! But alongside
production-focused nonprofits, the "société coopérative et
participative," and limited liability companies, they actively
contribute. LLCs have emerged as a practical model for platform
cooperatives, especially where worker or multi-stakeholder
cooperatives face legal or regulatory challenges. Recognized
across multiple jurisdictions and aligned with cooperative
principles, LLCs help platform co-ops to construct sustainable,
inclusive, and genuinely democratic digital platforms. While by
no means a "worker paradise," platform co-ops thrive as a
sustainable and socially responsible alternative to traditional
corporations.

The modern cooperative movement originated from the
realization that the global consumer economy, driven by the
wealthiest countries, was steering us toward climate catastrophe.
In response to the inherent "growth imperative" ingrained within
corporations, this movement vehemently advocated for reduced
energy consumption, waste generation, and greenhouse gas
emissions. Governments and the public have come to recognize
that cooperatives offer one of the most significant value propositions by providing an alternative to the growth imperative.
They contribute ideologically and concretely to the fight against
climate disaster. Cooperatives are fundamentally better positioned than traditional start-ups to combat climate change, as
evidenced by the example of Madagascar. This country, known
for its biodiversity and confronting significant environmental and
social challenges, has centered its transition to a cooperative
digital economy around regenerative agriculture and cooperative

platforms. The Tany Sambatra project, which translates to "beautiful land" in Malagasy, serves as a shining example of this approach.

Tany Sambatra establishes a regional second-level cooperative network, integrating farmers, their associations, and cooperatives through a centralized digital platform. By implementing practices such as agroforestry, soil conservation, crop diversification, water management, and collective data management, these small farmers aim to improve yields, income, and resilience to climate hazards. Another inspiring example is the Kerala Food Platform, which shows how other cooperatives are addressing the climate catastrophe.

According to Silicon Valley logic, entrepreneurial success is measured by building private companies worth billions. This approach, however, is not only challenging to achieve but also detrimental to workers and communities. Situated along the picturesque shores of the Arabian Sea in southern India, the Kerala Start-up Mission boldly challenges this prevailing narrative, shedding light on the stark contrast between the ethos of Gandhi or Marx and the tech titans of Silicon Valley. Kerala Start-up Mission advocates for India's state governments to support the development of tech start-ups based on sustainable business models that prioritize the well-being of workers, the environment, and society as a whole. There is also another important project in Kerala. Small farmers who belong to over 11,000 farm cooperatives faced challenges in selling their produce individually due to the inefficiency of transporting tiny quantities from their small-sized farms to the local market. But with the support of state government start-up funding, they came together to form a platform cooperative that aggregates farmers and collectively brings their produce to the market. By acting as a unified entity, these small farm cooperatives have gained a stronger market position, resulting in increased earnings and improved living standards for the farmers of Kerala.

Recognizing the pivotal role of cooperatives in tackling the climate crisis, policymakers in the United States have also begun actively promoting this model. Government assistance programs for platform co-ops have been established, alongside interagency working groups providing technology support for small and medium-sized businesses. I must commend the notable contributions of California governor Gavin Newsom and Colorado governor Jared Polis in shaping the landscape of gig work and cooperative expansion. Their administrations took significant strides by enacting laws to protect gig workers, ensuring they receive comparable benefits to traditional employment and limiting platform fees for fair income distribution. Moreover, they reduced the threshold for forming worker cooperatives, fostering the growth of cooperative ventures. This symbiotic relationship between the public and cooperatives proved to be mutually beneficial. Local governments recognized the essential role of cooperatives in delivering vital services and thus provided subsidies and regulatory assistance. This support not only bolstered local economies but also contributed to reducing the carbon footprint. The Polis and Newsom administrations implemented measures to promote the expansion of platform cooperatives, including exemptions from state cartel law restrictions and the establishment of digital cooperative mutual discount systems. They also offered cooperative growth incentives through tax benefits and grants. Billboards in major cities like Los Angeles and Denver played a crucial role in raising awareness among lawmakers and the general public, fostering collaboration between platform cooperatives at national and international levels.

By the year 2030, governments worldwide, from Spain to Bangladesh, recognized the political and economic advantages of supporting this shift toward cooperatives as a way to support climate justice. They have actively provided resources to these new platforms, responding also to the passionate advocacy of the global trade union network. This union network has emerged as a key proponent of worker-led platform cooperatives. In turn, this has led to the resurgence of many trade unions, reversing their previous decline in influence. Inspired by the leadership of Simel Esim, a Turkish American economist who has led the International Labour Organization's portfolio on cooperatives, the ILO, under the guidance of Secretary-General Gilbert F. Houngbo, has wholeheartedly taken up the cause of worker-led platform cooperatives. The ILO's efforts encompass various aspects, including the creation of open, interoperable infrastructure-governance models, rebalancing digital power through new organizations, and increasing public participation in data and technology policymaking.

Transitioning to the European Union, we find that the EU sought a distinct path, envisioning an internet that neither replicates the Chinese model nor blindly follows the American way. This vision holds great significance as transforming the infrastructure of the internet is essential alongside launching platform cooperatives. It is important to note that the European Commission's Digital Markets Act (DMA), introduced in September 2022, played a pivotal role in promoting competition in the digital economy. The DMA established rules for designated gatekeepers, imposing obligations to ensure fair treatment of users and competitors. Sanction mechanisms, including fines up to 10 percent of worldwide turnover, were implemented in cases of noncompliance.

Following the example of India, which adopted unified cooperative laws, the EU implemented a unified cooperative law in 2032, serving as a model for all member countries. Legal scholars also developed a platform co-op model law, influencing numerous nations. Governments gradually updated archaic cooperative laws and codes to reflect the increasingly democratic realities of the cooperative economy and the demand for a new regime of digital citizenship. These legal reforms addressed funding challenges faced by platform cooperatives, allowing them to access the same sources of capital as traditional businesses, including venture capital and private equity. Such reforms leveled the playing field, enabling platform co-ops to compete more effectively.

Another significant development is the rise of "smart cities" based on digital cooperative principles. The report highlights the work of Francesca Bria, Barcelona's chief technology and digital innovation officer, who has inspired cities worldwide to consider data sovereignty, particularly through city-run and city-supported taxi, e-scooter, and rental bicycle co-ops. Barcelona's city government is also involved in initiatives like Guifi Net, which brings cooperatively owned Wi-Fi services to those without internet access. This heightened awareness of data sovereignty has sparked transformative political and economic shifts, aligning with John Rawls's vision of a "property-owning democracy" where everyone has an equal stake in society. People have come to understand the need for alternatives that devolve power and restore it to workers and communities, reclaiming their agency.

Inspired by Bria's work, city governments have implemented policies to prevent complete private ownership and operation of digital urban infrastructure and associated data collection. For instance, autonomous vehicles used for public transportation, when implemented as proprietary entities, serve as a means to integrate technology into cities while democratizing the resulting data.

In 2035, we are fortunate to draw upon centuries of ideas and have the wind of cooperative history at our backs. An increasing number of individuals are embracing a pluralistic approach to effecting change, recognizing the potential of municipalism as a means to achieve immediate and long-term goals without neglecting the role of the federal government. This approach acknowledges the limitations of incremental changes at the federal level while appreciating the value of municipalism. Grassroots efforts for change are already making a tangible difference in cities worldwide.

One positive development is the growing interest in balancing local participation with centralized power to achieve democracy in the modern world. The individual nation-state is too large for meaningful involvement yet too small to address global issues. In this regard, the Rebel City Alliance emerged as a progressive league of cities and municipalities, including Kerala in India, Emilia-Romagna in Italy, the autonomous Basque region and Catalonia in Spain, New York City, and California. This alliance aims to expand and strengthen the movement by fostering networks among its members. These networks facilitate the exchange of data, tool kits, and financial templates that can be used across cities. They also enable municipalities to communicate policy successes across borders, collaborate on technological advancements, and harness the immense potential of their collective efforts.

These collaborations have resulted in municipalities implementing policies that give worker-owned businesses preferences in bidding through procurement mandates. Research has been funded to address legal hurdles faced by platform cooperatives, and specific social benefits have been provided to cooperative members. Lists of free or low-cost physical spaces have been created, and operating conditions have been improved. These mutually reinforcing policies have played a crucial role in the growth of the urban cooperative movement.

Beyond this, the book *Platform Socialism* by James Muldoon presents a thought-provoking argument about the undemocratic and extractive nature of existing platforms. Muldoon calls for a reconfiguration of these platforms to create a more equitable and just society. His vision of "platform cooperativism 2.0" combines the principles of cooperativism with the governance and resources of the public sector, aiming for a transformative and inclusive digital economy. In 2035, the concept of cooperatives as public utilities was thoroughly examined and explored. They serve as vital providers of essential services to communities, similar to traditional public utilities such as water, electricity, and telecommunications. And more and more, platform cooperatives have demonstrated their effectiveness in delivering services like rural and urban mobility, particularly in areas that conventional providers have not prioritized or shown interest in.

The ongoing project of transitioning to a more sustainable economy is a multifaceted and time-consuming process that will require many more years to complete. Building on the progress of the past half century, the movement should maintain a long-term perspective in pursuit of an environmentally sustainable, socially equitable, and economically prosperous society. This will call for more fundamental shifts in how we produce and consume goods and services.

It is crucial for the cooperative movement to continue building alliances with other social movements, including environmental-ists, unionists, food justice activists, feminists, social entrepreneurs, digital justice movement supporters, community technologists, and those involved in the public-interest tech movement. By collaborating and sharing templates for successful policies, these movements can amplify their impact, inspire change, and create a better future for all.

In 2035, the platform cooperative movement still thrives without a rigid ideological label. While some within the move-ment may argue against this approach, I am not one of them. The platform cooperative movement has always been open to all who support a democratic digital economy, whether they consider themselves socialists, privacy enthusiasts, open source and free culture quipsters, anarchists, remorseful invisible-hand admirers, or meaning-seeking Silicon Valley geeks. It is not exclusive to the left, nor should it be. The strength of the movement depends on people building co-ops tailored to their local needs and traditions, and in accordance with the wishes of their members. That said, I do believe the movement should proudly, unabashedly fly the flag of solidarity and social justice. The question is more about how to bring in the largest number and move it forward. However, what truly inspires me is the embrace of radical cooperative traditions within our local chapters, guided by the insights of figures such as Murray Bookchin, Noam Chomsky, W. E. B. Du Bois, Samir Amin, Gustavo Esteva, and Silvia Federici. Their work has propelled us to challenge systems of racism and colonialism and advocate for gender equality. Historically, cooperativism has always been a "big tent" movement under which diverse camps coexist. Ultimately, its successes owed more to pragmatism and flexibility than to a shared political creed. This remained essential also in 2035. Some co-ops are secular; others reflect spiritual values or religious beliefs.

At the same time, explicitly religious influences in co-ops are more prevalent than many realize. Throughout history, co-ops have been associated with spiritual leaders and movements. The Uralungal Labour Contract Co-operative Society in Kerala, India, was founded in close association with Vagbhatananda, a spiritual guru. The Kobe Cooperative in Japan was founded by Toyohiko Kagawa, a Christian reformer and labor activist. Mondragon, famously founded by Catholic priest José María Arizmendiarrieta, is deeply rooted in Basque and Catholic culture. Labels such as "socialist" would be rejected by many co-op aficionados.

As I transport you to the world of 2035, I am excited to also share new developments that have reshaped the technological landscape. In this near future, traditional financial systems, such

as M-Pesa, Western Union, and Wise, have been surpassed by
the minds of crypto visionaries hailing from Ghana, Cameroon,
and Nigeria. Their project, Send Globally, based on Bitcoin's
Lightning Network, has made the transfer of funds easier,
enabling secure and borderless transactions for migrating
workers, granting users greater control over their funds.

The ICA's project of a "co-op phone" had great impact. It
involved coordinating co-ops globally to collectively purchase
millions of smartphones preloaded with international platform
co-op apps, produced in Shenzhen, facilitating cost-effective
connectivity and transcending geographical barriers. This
initiative really changed how co-ops connect, enabling meaningful connections, governance, and collaboration on a global scale.
In 2030, the International Cooperative Alliance (ICA) expanded
the seven cooperative principles to include environmental sustainability as the eighth principle. There were also deliberations
regarding proactive diversity, a more lenient approach to partnering with municipalities, and data sovereignty as potential
additions to the cooperative principles.

In the same year, the ICA launched the Digital Youth
Catalysts campaign, focusing on inclusive economic prospects in
the platform economy and supporting global platform cooperative incubators with a special focus on youth, emphasizing
renewable energy, sustainable transportation, climate resilience,
water and waste management, and inclusive urban planning.

A year later, a significant milestone was achieved by the
cooperative movement with the introduction of a global cooperative identity, CoopID—similar to OpenID—and the declaration
of FairCoin as the global cryptocurrency for cooperatives,
allowing easy payment through the "co-op phone." FairCoin,
launched in 2014, emerged as a digital currency dedicated to
fairness, social justice, and environmental sustainability within
the decentralized FairCoop ecosystem. With the active

involvement and stewardship of the ICA, FairCoin has solidified its position as the preferred cryptocurrency for co-ops, freeing them from the excessive transaction fees imposed by major payment networks; FairCoin enables seamless and cost-effective transactions.

Also coordinated by the ICA, the Cooperative Data Standards Association (CDCA) promotes data interoperability among cooperatives and other solidarity economy companies, fostering a fair digital economy. As a central repository of resources, the association facilitates collaboration and streamlines business operations.

Simultaneously, the once-dominant social media platforms, including Facebook, Twitter, MySpace, AOL Instant Messenger, Orkut, and Vine, have faded into obscurity. Mark Zuckerberg's ambitious foray into the metaverse, alongside Apple's attempts, ultimately met with failure as these companies prioritized profit over the genuine needs and desires of their users. This led to a profound disillusionment with the tech industry, igniting a quest for alternative technological approaches. Users disengaged from the sale of their "behavioral surplus" and the manipulation of nonmarket behavioral data, as American scholar and author Shoshana Zuboff astutely described, resulting in a growing discontent with the industry.

In this transformed digital landscape, a new paradigm of online sociality has emerged. Enter the independent "social media brigades": self-sustaining groups that nurture digital spaces, facilitate meaningful conversations, and ensure the free flow of information. Each brigade manifests its unique cloud infrastructure, reflecting the distinct interests, needs, and values of its members. Together, they form a vast network of decentralized social spaces that breathe life into the digital realm. Moreover, the recent report by the World Economic Forum acknowledges the imperative of a new public infrastructure for the internet and social media, an idea that was once considered radical but has now found its rightful place in the spotlight.

Germany and the UK have embarked on initial endeavors to build public social media platforms, echoing the legacy of public broadcast companies in their respective nations, such as ARD/ ZDF and the BBC. These initiatives reflect the collective recognition of the need for a new decentralized social media paradigm that values public interest.

In 2035, the fediverse has emerged as a notable model that captivates attention and garners' widespread adoption. It represents a decentralized network of interconnected social media platforms that have changed the digital landscape. Led by autonomous small servers like People Link, May First, and Greenhost, the fediverse has assisted users with unparalleled control over their digital communications and data. This transformative shift has allowed users to reclaim agency, shaping their own digital experiences according to their values and aspirations. Notably, the advent of "feminist servers" has addressed the need for secure access, data protection, and the management of feminist initiatives, fostering an environment that supports women's autonomy, security, and inclusivity. Brazilian collective Vedetas exemplifies the power of the fediverse in nurturing feminist technologies, enhancing online activities, and building an inclusive digital space.

The emergence of the new fediverse harkens back to the early social experiments on the internet, reminiscent of the sense of community and sociality that characterized the era. Howard Rheingold's book *The Virtual Community* beautifully illustrates the influence of the WELL, a renowned online community from the 1980s known for its focus on discussion, collaboration, and shared interests. The new fediverse signifies a profound shift toward an internet that is more inclusive and user-centric. Over the years, it has undergone remarkable transformations propelled by the shared vision of its users and the diligent efforts of developers. User-friendly interfaces and intuitive features have attracted a wider user base, making the fediverse accessible to individuals of varying technological proficiency levels. Additionally, decentralized moderation mechanisms have expanded, allowing communities to shape content moderation policies based on user-driven values and ethical guidelines. This ensures that the platform remains aligned with the principles and aspirations of its diverse user base.

Also fans of popular platforms like Twitch and Roblox have taken matters into their own hands. They have established their own cooperative-based platforms, where the majority of revenue no longer flows into the pockets of intermediaries. No longer do they give 75 percent of their earnings to Roblox, or 50 percent to Twitch. Enough! These fan-driven initiatives have reshaped the landscape of digital entertainment, fostering a sense of ownership among content creators and consumers alike.

Amid the surge of collective alternatives, a remarkable wave of global dating apps has emerged, embodying a different ethos within the cooperative movement. CoopCupid, SolidarityMatch, and CoopWhisper are among the pioneers offering a refreshing alternative to the competitive dating culture depicted in Gary Shteyngart's novel *Super Sad True Love Story*. These innovative dating "co-opy" apps prioritize authentic connections based on shared values, long-term goals, and empathy, shifting the focus away from superficial attributes like attractiveness, net worth, and social media popularity. As CoopCupid user Maria from Curitiba in Brazil stressed, these cooperative dating apps provide a much-needed departure from the judgmental nature of a competitive, exclusionary dating culture, as portrayed in Shteyngart's novel.

We are also witnessing a historic surge of activity as disenchanted designers and technologists from major tech firms join the burgeoning cooperative movement. Dozens, then hundreds, and eventually thousands of brilliant minds have departed from the allure of Big Tech, redirecting their talents toward the cooperative endeavors that prioritize collective welfare over corporate profits. The exodus from established tech giants like Google can be attributed to various factors. Dissatisfaction with the implementation of AI, monetization of user data, and concerns over privacy have propelled these talented individuals to seek alternatives that align with their ethical principles. Joining cooperative tech was simply more meaningful.

With the increasing popularity of platform cooperatives, and a recognition of their contribution to the fight against the climate catastrophe, a shift toward more acceptance has occurred within universities. More scholars recognize that workers and communities possess their own visions and transformative power. They now understand that, let's say, impoverished immigrants have the capability to effectively run tech platforms. Thus, the cooperative business model infiltrates curricula across the globe, from high school textbooks to leading universities' economics departments, and a new generation of graduates emerges. These graduates, influenced by cooperative education, assume roles as elected officials, legal scholars, and advocates, with the power to amend outdated laws that have hindered the growth of the cooperative economy.

Following the largest strikes in higher education in United States history in 2029, with tens of thousands of academic and administrative workers striking across the country, new forms of universities became infinitely more attractive. This newfound acceptance has led to the emergence of hybrid cooperative-public colleges, modeled after the platform co-op framework. The establishment of the Global Center for Advanced Studies in Dublin in April 2018, as the first co-owned degree-granting institution of higher education, paved the way for these hybrid platform co-ops. Other roots include the International Center for

Co-operative Management at the Sobey School of Business in Canada, while the Cooperative University of Kenya became an inspiring force in educating leaders in Africa's growing cooperative movement. Building on this history, these new degree-granting colleges have reshaped the landscape of higher education, offering a robust alternative to conventional models. Through shared governance and collective ownership, they have become multi-stakeholder cooperatives firmly rooted in cooperative principles. They teach mostly online, but students also meet in cafes, pubs, homes, and museums. The state or municipality holds noncontrolling shares in these platform co-ops, ensuring the institutions remain grounded in their mission. It worked! These colleges emerged as pioneers, federating and pooling faculty and learning resources across institutions, while embodying and teaching cooperative principles. They have redefined higher education. They function as self-managed cooperative entities, with departments structured as self-governing worker cooperatives. At People's CoopU in Athens, Greece, for instance, decision-making extends beyond a limited board of trustees. "At People's CoopU, we are using digital learning platforms that are open-source or cooperatively owned. It was about time!" said Dimitris, a student at People's CoopU. In this new educational landscape, instructors have embraced a fresh role as learning coaches, opening the doors also for nontraditional faculty with unconventional credentials. The traditional course system, once rigid and linear, has evolved into vibrant learning "units." These units, spanning from brief two-hour modules to comprehensive three-year programs, cater to the diverse needs of learners beyond the confines of traditional academia. Retired professionals, high schoolers, middle schoolers, and all those seeking knowledge beyond conventional boundaries have found their place in this innovative approach. These new educational institutions draw extensively from open educational materials like the WikimediaCommons and Project Gutenberg. They prioritize the commons, ensuring that their research output is shared openly for the benefit of the public. It's a cornerstone of their mission.

As I conclude this letter, I acknowledge that while recent years have brought about a transformative wave, our insurrection remains partial. Platform cooperatives are neither universally applicable nor understood. In the so-called Global South, more than 3 billion people still lack access to basic internet service, let alone high-speed connectivity, and ambitious projects like Alphabet's Loon have failed to address this issue. The first priority for many families is to provide sustenance for their families, and after that, they prioritize the education of their children. And it is only then that maybe they can think about the potentials of platform cooperatives. For women, the feasibility of such endeavors, however, often also depends on patriarchal structures that grant only men control over devices in the household. We must recognize that the fight for a fair and democratic internet must also be a struggle for basic human rights, food safety, gender equality, health care, and education (digital literacy and otherwise) within our communities. When your pantry is as empty as your stomach, immediate needs outweigh concerns about data privacy or the apps-based economy. To build a co-op is to challenge old ways of thinking about "property" and "development" and contribute to new narratives about community rights, sustainable development, and the satisfaction of basic human needs. This narrative can never be a finished story but must be continually written, and updated, by its millions of authors.

The time to start this work is now. The biggest difference between 2023 and 2035 is that large co-op organizations are clearer about their responsibility to support international platform co-ops and coordinate and govern data, especially in low-income countries, where hope is too often in short supply. We want to provide the tools that enable people and communities to believe in their power, their economic value, and their economic rights. I believe it is within our grasp to build and nurture an ecosystem of alternative solutions to platform capitalism by 2050. Is this goal daunting? Yes. Is it impossible? No. We simply need to continue building out the necessary infrastructure: data commons, international platform co-ops, payment and government systems, social media, and distribution networks.

At the same time, we must push forward in the development of new business models compatible with the earth's ecosystem and its natural limits. This means finding new measures of value besides GDP and wealth creation, a currency more important than dollars and euros. Luckily, there are already millions of people around the world committed to this vision and working on the kinds of projects needed to realize it. If we unite, and pool all of our technological and intellectual resources, we can build, at last, a world in accordance with Robert Owen's foundational insight. "There is but one mode by which man can possess in perpetuity all the happiness which his nature is capable of enjoying," wrote Owen. "That is by the union and co-operation of all for the benefit of each."

In Solidarity,
Trebor Scholz

Epilogue:
How to Start a Platform Co-op

In 2019, after speaking at a conference in Brasília, I made a quick visit to Belo Horizonte, the capital of the southern state of Minas Gerais and Brazil's third-largest city. Upon disembarking at the airport, I was immediately confronted by a colossal billboard for Uber, the global ride-sharing behemoth. The company's logo followed me through the city, with Uber ads covering countless commercial surfaces, and stickers with the company's name adorning countless windshields. It felt like the company had achieved full-market saturation, with the city under a blanket of advertising, unlike anything I had seen in the United States. This was true on roads that passed Portuguese-style villas, as well as those going through favelas thick with shacks of corrugated metal and brick. Uber was in command of the roads across the city's hilly terrain, and of its winding streets and canyons that during sunset reminded me of San Francisco by way of Stuttgart.

I visited the Coopertáxi offices on one of Belo's steep hill streets, Rua Pitangui. They were located behind the blue-tiled facade of a concrete building that had seen better days, but proudly displayed the company's logo, which featured the international co-op emblem, two pine trees. The pine tree has long been associated with virility and endurance. The co-op symbol of two pine trees represents cooperation. Their trunks rise from roots that form a circle, representing the global ecosystem, which depends on cooperation to survive.

At Coopertáxi, I was greeted by a smiling young woman wearing the co-op's light blue uniform and ushered into a modest-sized call center on the first floor. Inside, four or five similarly uniformed employees took calls and matched each rider with one of the co-op's 400 licensed drivers.

The co-op's president, Clauber Marcos Borges, explained to me with evident, if extremely formal, satisfaction that Coopertáxi had been founded in 1984, making it one of the oldest taxi co-ops in Belo Horizonte. "We are in our thirty-fourth year and we've had a lot of success up until this point," he proclaimed. "Our cooperative has 438 worker-owners and 50 staff members in our call center and administrative offices [who] accept around 130,000 rides per month. We simply love technology and embrace it. Our plan is to expand our cooperative with a technological solution. Because our app accounts for 60 percent of the 130,000 rides per month, we have reduced the size of our call center by half."

Despite Borges's confidence and pleasure in the progress of the co-op, the truth is, I was worried for them. Very worried. We talked about how they might compete with the estimated 10,000 drivers in the city using the major ride-hailing apps, especially since Uber had begun actively recruiting the unemployed. Coopertáxi was vehemently opposed to hiring unlicensed, unemployed drivers, believing that customers would prefer drivers who looked more professional, wearing the blue and white uniform of their cooperative.

The co-op instead responded to competition by offering a 30 percent discount to passengers. This significantly increased business, but such steep discounts are not sustainable. How would they compete when customers became more concerned with low prices? What technologies would they use to update their business model? What was their founding story? How would they match

Uber's marketing effort? And did passengers really care enough about uniforms or taxi licenses?

The questions hanging over Coopertáxi amid Uber's onslaught in Belo Horizonte were not unique. Co-ops around the world face challenges, sometimes existential ones, that they are not always equipped to meet or think through fully. All co-ops are, to an extent, works in progress and continuing experiments in alternative models for organizing society.

As such, there can be no permanent rulebooks and handbooks, though Johnston Birchall's 1988 book *Co-op: the People's Business* and *The Oxford Handbook of Mutual, Co-operative, and Co-owned Business* have offered useful guidance on principles for running cooperatives. Given the rapid pace of technological, social, and economic change, the forces shaping every co-op's operating environment are never static for long. Primers must be constantly refreshed, new lessons added to the centuries-long tradition of theorizing co-op principles and goals.

To this end, I humbly present select lessons and observations— some general, others specific—made over the course of writing this book. I offer them in the hope they can help new-generation platform co-ops take root, and help older ones incorporate new technologies and adapt to changing times. To avoid appearing selective in my comments, I have largely refrained from naming individual cooperatives.

Story

In the beginning, there is a story. A compelling origin narrative is crucial for the founding team of any digital platform. Storytelling is the simplest way to capture and hold people's attention. For a platform co-op, you will need an energizing and intriguing origin story. Most likely, you already have one, even if you aren't aware of it. You may not be aware of your biggest strength. When settling on a narrative, ask for feedback on how your founding story compares to others'. You may be surprised at how well it is received—or by how much work is needed to give it the resonance that will persuade people to support your project.

Communication may seem like a soft skill compared to the challenges of cooperative governance, Greg Brodsky of Start.coop emphasizes, but it is essential for promoting and engaging others in your cooperative. At the core, a co-op should be able to clearly answer fundamental questions such as why they exist, who owns the business, and what it does. Clear and concise communication is crucial in conveying these ideas to various audiences.[1]

Business First

In an economy where many feel powerless, a platform co-op provides an opportunity to regain agency and contribute something meaningful. The well-known adage "culture eats strategy for breakfast," coined by management consultant and writer Peter Drucker, stresses the importance of cultivating a strong organizational culture. While it may not be entirely accurate to say that a "business eats cooperative culture for lunch," the two are undoubtedly interconnected. The launch of a cooperative is an exciting event filled with hope and possibility, but even the best bylaws and shared belief in democratic processes may not prevent it from running out of money. The appeal of starting a platform co-op lies in building a sense of community and identity, as well as a strong business venture; to ensure success, an initial focus on building a strong business model is key.

While it's commendable that some platform cooperatives devote significant time to composing manifestos, declaring their stance on labor rights and distinguishing themselves from competitors, it's essential to keep in mind that these are still businesses that must survive in the long run. Knowing how to distribute revenue is essential, but equally important is having the knowledge and strategies to generate revenue in the first place. While declaring a distinct set of principles is important as a symbolic act, platform cooperatives must also concentrate on creating sustainable and profitable business models in order to continue providing services and having a positive impact.

Cooperative Culture

Many people have heard about cooperative culture, but they may not comprehend what it entails until they see it in action. Most platform co-ops do not originate from a single entrepreneur who brings together a group; instead, they start as a group that must learn to work together and become a team. Cooperative culture places cooperation at the center and involves self-aware and giving teamwork with a shared purpose. This culture prioritizes cooperation, democratic decision-making, equality, and mutual support, and places the collective well-being of the members over individual gain. Although a genuine cooperative culture may be unfamiliar to most, there are some countries and regions where cooperatives and the spirit of cooperation are integrated into their educational systems, introducing children to these values and practices from a young age. Even in these places, however, cooperative culture must be actively taught and cultivated over and over, emphasizing its importance and promoting it through workshops and discussions. Even in the meccas of cooperativism, a true understanding of cooperative culture cannot be taken for granted. It is crucial not to view cooperative culture as a peripheral but rather as a fundamental component of any successful platform cooperative that needs to be taught and learned. During the Platform Cooperativism Consortium conference in Rio de Janeiro, a leader of the Team Academy at Mondragon University highlighted a crucial point: "We don't create cooperatives, we create cooperative people."

Leadership for All

Platform co-ops are prompting a reconsideration of the cultural obsession with the visionary solo entrepreneur and traditional leadership models. Co-ops are sometimes thought of as leaderless and associated with the saying, attributed to Oscar Wilde, that "the trouble with socialism is that it takes up too many evenings." Democratic processes, while important for ensuring fairness and inclusivity, can also be slower and lead to a perception that co-ops are slower to act. But in reality, most platform co-ops (like most other co-ops) do have distinct leaders. The org chart of platform cooperatives looks different but they don't have to be "a mess" in terms of management, despite what corporate zealots with limited understanding of cooperatives may believe. These are people who have the ability or resources to play a bigger role in assisting the process, even in the most democratic worker cooperatives. These leaders are not terrifying, all-powerful managers or office tyrants, to start with; they simply *preside* over the co-op, they implement the rules that the collective has shaped. Unlike corporate executives, these leaders are accountable to the workers and they can be—and are on occasion—removed by them. This accountability creates a fundamentally different dynamic based on lateral collaboration.

Co-op leadership, like that in any other business, is susceptible to burnout. Motivated founders may push themselves too hard in pursuit of worthy goals, and they may overly identify themselves with their venture. Platform co-op leaders need to exercise self-care and, importantly, recognize that they are not their company. Some cooperatives have even been known to survive on self-exploitation, so such behaviors must be resisted. Some founders who could afford it have even taken a full year off to recuperate before returning to their co-op.

There are also other models. Team entrepreneurship, some-times known as "teampreneurship," an approach that was pioneered in Finland, is gaining popularity in the solidarity economy com-munity. It refers to a group of people that work together with a shared purpose and only minimal wage disparity. In contrast to most traditional corporate leadership, teampreneurship is not hier-archical; it is built on the collective strength of the team. Mondragon University's MTA Labs use a "teampreneurship" approach to busi-ness education. Students gain hands-on experience in all aspects of management and learn problem-solving, critical thinking, and conflict resolution skills. Teampreneurship involves taking risks and working toward a shared goal with a focus on economic, environmental, social, and spiritual dimensions. MTA's team-preneurship education is linked to rotating leadership, encouraging self-organizing individuals to take initiative and granting team members creative flexibility to learn and grow together, which is often lacking in corporate settings.

Katherine Sobering's book, *The People's Hotel: Working for Justice in Argentina*, provides insights into the rotating leadership approach of Hotel Bauen, a worker cooperative that operated a luxury hotel in Buenos Aires for a decade during the early 2000s. Workers at the hotel, including housekeepers, receptionists, book-keepers, cooks, and bartenders, rotated through various roles to avoid burnout and encourage skill development. Despite ulti-mately closing, the decade-long operation of Hotel Bauen as a worker cooperative demonstrated that dividing roles can foster teamwork, skill development, and a sustainable and healthy work environment. While rotating leadership is not yet a widespread practice among platform co-ops, it could greatly benefit them by allowing team members to rely on each other's strengths and foster trust and communication within the group.

Starting with the Right People

When it comes to building a successful business, it is often said, you need to start with the right people. And for platform co-op founders, this means starting with the people they want to end up with. If social justice and diversity is the mission, this should be reflected in the team makeup from day one. Small founding teams with a shared purpose and diverse skill sets tend to be the most innovative. However, forming a cooperative team based on shared ideals or friendships rather than complementary expertise can lead to ineffective teamwork. Sometimes, a group of friends may have a good idea and secure funding for it, but that doesn't necessarily mean they are the right team to execute that idea. Successful co-ops require both a shared purpose and diverse skill sets.

A diverse team brings different perspectives, experiences, and skills to the table, each of which can help you achieve your goals better. If you want to end up with a team that includes minoritized people, you should start with one. A team that is representative of the community you want to serve can help build trust and credibility. Having a team representative of the community being served can help build trust and credibility. In short, building a successful platform co-op starts with building the right team from the beginning.

Joining an Existing Social Franchise or Federation vs. Starting from Scratch

Starting a business involves deciding whether to start from scratch or join an existing franchise or federation. Joining an existing one has advantages like access to shared digital infrastructure, replicating an existing proven model, and being part of a supportive community for networking opportunities. By taking an internationalist approach, cooperatives can share resources, expertise, and best practices, creating a more level playing field for platform co-ops to compete with large global enterprises. Being an internationalist may place you outside of your comfort zone when it comes to overcoming language and cultural differences. In the short term, it may be more convenient for you to find your tech team locally. But such a local approach may limit access to the resources and support that larger federations can provide, which is crucial in the long run as small local tech shops may not have the same level of resources and ongoing support.

Starting a business from scratch can be challenging, especially when your local circumstances are unique and may not be transferable to other places, co-ops, or countries. However, in the "Platform Co-ops Now!" course, we found that dozens of the 1,300 students from over sixty countries expressed interest in starting short-term rental, food delivery, or ride-hailing platforms in their local areas. Surprisingly, the default assumption for many was that they had to develop their software from scratch. Furthermore, trying to build a platform and create governance structures from scratch can be time-consuming, expensive, and risky.

Platform cooperatives in low-income countries, especially those run by women, often face greater barriers to success in the tech industry. That's why Señoritas Couriers in São Paulo, a platform co-op for Black LGBTQIAP+ women, considers joining CoopCycle. Embracing an internationalist approach and being open to replication and social franchising can help co-ops stay focused on their core mission and values, rather than becoming overwhelmed with technical and administrative details. In Latin America and beyond, platform cooperatives will look very different; they'll focus on providing access to essential services such as health care and education, which are often lacking in these countries.

Platform co-ops in Africa may use SMS-based services due to high mobile phone ownership and limited internet access. In India, hyperlocal apps designed for a single village may be successful.[2] Co-ops designed to serve women and other marginalized groups may also emerge through South-South collaborations. Despite the variations and unique characteristics of each local context, joining an established cooperative federation or platform often proves to be the most favorable choice, as it grants access to shared digital infrastructure and resources.

Entrepreneurial Wayfinding

There is no one-size-fits-all option for launching a platform co-op, as the best approach will vary depending on needs, available resources, and country. Before starting their own platform co-op, however, all prospective entrepreneurs should keep a few things in mind.

Prospective co-op founders should keep in mind that not all founding journeys are the same. CooperativesUK's UnFound program, for example, offers a development tool called the Founder Journey for budding platform co-op entrepreneurs in the UK.[3]

The journey begins with a solid team of co-founders with the right skills to tackle challenges. Define your co-op's purpose and business model and identify stakeholders such as members, workers, suppliers, and clients. Then choose the best cooperative structure for your needs.

Consider forming a worker cooperative if you want to give workers ownership and governance, which can foster a greater sense of control and commitment. Multi-stakeholder and worker co-ops are a good choice for promoting social justice, but you should also decide whether you want the people who use your services to be members, such as those who receive your care or stream your music. Keep in mind that worker co-ops require worker engagement, meaning that everyone on the team needs to be fully committed.

As you make your decision, it's a good idea to start building a social media presence to raise awareness of your co-op and attract potential members. Once you have defined your business strategy and chosen your cooperative structure, the next steps include assembling your board and registering your co-op. This is also a great opportunity to launch a microsite, to start creating low-cost prototypes, and to recruit users to test them.

The next step, according to UnFound, is securing your first funds, which can be achieved through grants, loans, or investments based on your business case. Start.coop, a US-based organization, adds that a business strategy that has validation by the community is crucial to demonstrate to funders that you can deliver on your ambitions.

Next, build your core team and specify your internal operations. Launch a rewards-based crowdfunding campaign and create a minimal viable product. Start accepting new members and generating revenue. Once you've assigned clear roles in your organization and built your profile, scaling the business may become an option, but it requires additional members and revenue. Carefully weigh the risks and rewards of scaling before making a decision.

Funding

Securing start-up funding for platform cooperatives, although more challenging than for VC-funded start-ups, is still possible through various options. Worker-owned platform cooperatives can sell shares to workers, but this method is not commonly used to raise significant funds. Crowdfunding is an effective pathway for platform co-ops where all stakeholders benefit. Philanthropy, government and especially municipal grants, loans (especially from cooperative banks), and outside investments are also possible sources of funding. Some successful platform cooperatives have even accepted outside capital while retaining control of their business.

Start.coop's Brodksy emphasizes that paying worker-members adequately as soon as possible is a crucial component of long-term viability. Yes, people idealistically support the growth and survival of platform co-ops, but they must also pay their rent or mortgage, cover day-care expenses, and put away retirement savings. The team, their time spent working on the co-op, and the intellectual property they represent are likely to be among your most valuable assets. You should avoid putting them in a position where they must choose between their own financial stability and participation in the co-op. As rapidly as feasible, pay the team a competitive wage.[4]

The 2019 Nesta Foundation report "Platform Co-operatives Solving the Capital Conundrum" suggests using social impact bonds and community shares to raise patient, value-aligned risk capital. With the right mix of funding, the report argues, platform co-ops have the potential to create a more equitable economy.

Platform co-ops may not receive venture capital backing like typical Silicon Valley start-ups, but this is also true for the vast majority of tech start-ups. Impact venture capitalists are more likely to fund traditional start-ups with significant market returns. Therefore, developing a community of like-minded individuals who are passionate about the issue at hand is crucial for platform cooperatives, and considering the option of noncontrolling shares from investors can be a topic of discussion in this regard.

Incorporation

Choosing the right location for incorporating your start-up is crucial. Look for regions with a strong infrastructure for supporting co-ops, like Kerala, Emilia-Romagna, New Zealand, the Basque

Country, Finland, or Kenya. In the United States, Colorado and Wisconsin have favorable legislation for platform co-ops. However, some platform co-ops, such as Stocksy United, have chosen to relocate to more conducive locations, like Vancouver in Canada, due to the legal and regulatory environment for their specific business.

Choosing a supportive location is crucial for the success of a platform cooperative. Look for regions dense with co-ops and a strong infrastructure to support them. Consider the availability of resources, such as funding, networking opportunities, and educational programs, as well as the municipality's attitude toward co-ops. In areas with unfavorable policy environments, consider establishing a limited liability company, or LLC, instead.

Platform co-ops in the United States and other parts of the world often operate as limited liability companies, even if they refer to themselves as worker cooperatives. While starting a worker-owned and -operated co-op may be ideal, it is not always possible due to legal, cultural, and political barriers. In some African countries, for example, co-ops may be associated with corruption. It is important to be aware of such challenges and to explore alternative structures that can still uphold cooperative principles.

The LLC model has grown in popularity among small businesses in recent years, and it's easy to see why. The flexibility of the LLC form allows founders to tailor the structure of their business to their specific needs. For example, they can be set up to allow for different types of membership, and they can be crafted into platform co-ops. The flexibility of the LLC model should be used to further worker-owned and operated businesses.

But incorporation as a cooperative is frequently portrayed as the sole goal. Too often, co-op supporters, union leaders, or advocates get caught up in the debate over which organizational model and technology is best. Co-ops, unions, ESOPS, DAOs, and so forth, all have their proponents and detractors. What matters most, however, is not the form of the organization or the tech solution, but the results it achieves for people. A near-religious, tunnel-vision commitment to the advancement of a single model does not help. "Human beings come first, then come cooperatives," as Mondragon's founder Arizmendiarrieta liked to say. Rephrased, we could say that the well-being of people should be the top priority, and cooperatives are a means to achieve it. Ultimately, the success of any organizational model should be measured by its ability to improve people's lives, regardless of whether it takes the form of a co-op, a union, or any other structure.

Co-Design

"Build it and they will come" is a popular saying among start-up entrepreneurs, but it's often inaccurate. A group of charismatic activists with great design skills aimed to build an ecosystem of platform co-ops in their city but faced issues as they did not consider the needs of local communities. Their experience emphasizes the significance of involving all stakeholders from the outset. Many platform co-op founders focus on addressing the needs of marginalized or underserved communities, but in any case it is important to ensure that there is a genuine need for the platform being developed. Engaging with potential stakeholders from the start and designing the platform with their needs in mind can help ensure its success.

Engage stakeholders in the design process to ensure community buy-in for platform cooperatives. Unlike VC-funded startups, co-ops typically include members of their intended user community, aligning the organization's purpose with the community it serves. Without proper engagement and co-design, start-ups are likely to fail.

Peer Production Licenses

While cooperatives have the potential to safeguard and generate commons, they frequently fall short of this ideal, which is also reflected in the sixth cooperative principle. Platform cooperatives, like most co-ops, frequently operate under a copyright system, using proprietary software. Besides that, rather than opening up to the global community, some cooperatives are occasionally self-enclosed around their membership.[5] When it comes to software, the options range from open/free/libre source, source available, and proprietary. In the early stages of a business, it can be challenging for platform co-op entrepreneurs to develop a fully value-aligned product. Several founders, therefore, have leveraged peer production licenses. Popular peer production licenses include CopyLeft and Creative Commons Plus.

Here is how they work: a peer production license for source-available software is used by platform co-ops such as CoopCycle to limit the commercial use of software to worker cooperatives, for example. One benefit of peer production licenses is that they can shield cooperatives from abuse by corporate competitors. As a result, these licenses have had a significant impact, in encouraging cooperatives to release their code without fear of appropriation by incumbents.

Drivers Cooperative founders initially found themselves using commercial, proprietary software that did not align well with their values.[6] When this New York City–based, 9,000-driver-strong platform co-op launched in May 2020, it paid $6,000 for the code of an "Uber clone" that they could use and modify but not publish as open source.[7] It was still far from ideal after being modified to meet their needs, but it was sufficient to get started and grow their business. The co-op grew and in 2020 temporarily switched to the Access-a-Ride service, which was initiated as a pilot project in

1980 in New York City following a lawsuit against the Metropolitan Transportation Authority for failing to provide adequate support to people with disabilities, and has since become a vital service for 144,000 New Yorkers who are unable to walk, making some 6 million trips per year.[8] The Drivers Cooperative initially became profitable by using basic software but later transitioned to a more competitive model by re-coding their app. While not applicable to all industries, the example of Drivers Cooperative highlights that it is possible to save hundreds of thousands of dollars by adopting a simple, cost-effective approach to owning basic code and software, rather than writing code from scratch or purchasing expensive white-label software.

When launching a business, it's wise to be mindful of your financial resources and start with a lighter-weight technology. Consider your core requirements on day one and partner with existing platforms or rent technology to get started without breaking the bank. Remain flexible and adaptable, knowing that your feature set and design will likely change multiple times as you grow. In the early stages, focus on the core functions of the business and put grander plans aside. Lastly, remember to politely decline pro-bono offers to develop your website during a weekend hackathon.

Are Blockchains Right for You?

The blockchain industry is often associated with fraudsters, but there is a growing community of developers creating impressive Web3 projects that can make a difference. While scams still exist, there are opportunities for those who pursue crypto projects. However, the decision to build on blockchain is not straightforward.

Blockchains like Ethereum are often hailed as groundbreaking innovations that have the potential to revolutionize a wide range of industries. When contemplating whether to use blockchain technology for your cooperative, however, it's crucial to move beyond the hype and evaluate the potential benefits. It's essential to determine if there are any functional blockchain projects in your industry and weigh the pros and cons of alternative coding options before making a decision. Additionally, including these considerations allows for an informed decision. While buzzwords such as "blockchain" may help with grant applications and give a first-mover advantage, if funds are limited, blockchains may not be the best fit for your cooperative.

Deciding Who Decides

There are many cooperative governance models, each with its own advantages and drawbacks. In the direct democracy model, each member of the co-op has a say in all decisions, while in the representative democracy model, members elect representatives to make decisions on their behalf. The former model could be too time-consuming for large cooperatives to implement, and it also opens up to the "tyranny of the majority" problem where the preferences of the many could be imposed on the few. In a representative democracy, used by most platform co-ops, members elect representatives to make decisions on their behalf. There are macro decisions such as organizational strategy and micro decisions such as day-to-day operations. In order to prevent excessive bureaucracy, it is frequently necessary to delegate micro-decisions; nevertheless, this delegation must be balanced with the need for collaborative macro-decision making. For example, in a food cooperative, the board might delegate the decision of what new products to carry to a committee, but the whole membership would need to vote on whether to open a new location. Direct democracy can lead to more engaged members, but representative democracy can be more efficient. The key is finding the right balance for your cooperative.

Many platform cooperatives use "sociocracy" as a form of governance that aims to promote equality and transparency in the decision-making process. It involves grouping members into circles, each with their own duties and responsibilities. These circles make choices using consent-based decision-making, in which objections are addressed and resolved in order to obtain a proposal that is acceptable to all members.

Committees and assemblies in cooperatives are another good way of creating a sense of ownership and participation among members. This becomes particularly important in larger cooperatives or globally distributed platform co-ops where it's easy to feel disconnected. Such committees and assemblies can help facilitate a more inclusive and collaborative decision-making process, where members can volunteer and become more involved in the work of the co-op over time. This model promotes shared responsibility among members, fostering a deeper sense of community and collaboration, rather than focusing solely on the election of a few cooperative leaders.

Fallibility

It's no secret that start-up life is no easy feat. Launching and maintaining an upstart is difficult, with challenges such as funding and the possibility of failure. While it is commonly known that 90 percent of Silicon Valley start-ups fail, cooperatives face even tougher odds. However, co-ops fail for similar reasons as regular businesses do: poor business models, flawed implementation, lack of skill or experience, and insufficient funding and time. It is important to learn from failures and celebrate the lessons they provide. Cooperatives should embrace failure as an opportunity for learning and growth, drawing inspiration from the Japanese art of *kintsugi*, which mends broken pottery with gold. Platform co-ops embrace fallibility as a continuous circle of iteration, of experimentation, of learning from what works.

Out of the Shadows

Cooperatives have a political dimension, despite being known for their collective self-help efforts. Co-ops hold a unique position in nurturing an economy built on principles of equity, and in doing so, they inherently contribute to the advancement of political aspirations. Our every action is political. Silence on political matters implies complicity with the prevailing power structures, as no one truly stands outside the political landscape. When you use a cultural inversion machine and place unions at the top, you could end up with cooperatives at the bottom, as they tend to be more introverted and may not project their values outward. Cooperatives should project their values outward, collaborate with political parties and movements, and even consider forming co-op parties or joining larger national and global movements to promote equity and justice, while also maintaining financial independence from foundations, government, and philanthropy. It's time for us to step out of the shadows, embrace our responsibility, and actively shape our future through the choices we make.

Acknowledgments

I would like to extend my gratitude to everyone in this movement for their daily efforts to make the world a more dignified, humane, and livable place. You give me hope. With heartfelt appreciation, I acknowledge especially the people I've interviewed, each demonstrating a deep commitment to promoting worker ownership in the digital economy.

My special thanks goes out to Leo Hollis and Jeanne Tao at Verso for their encouragement and astute input. I also owe a tremendous debt of gratitude to the Berggruen Institute, the Open Society Foundations, and the Berkman Klein Center for Internet and Society at Harvard University for their generous support, both in terms of fellowships and intellectual community. Beyond this, I am immensely thankful to Jose Mari Luzarraga Monasterio and Aitor Lizartza Martín for inviting me to be in residence at Mondragon University, where I had the opportunity to broaden my understanding of cooperative culture. At my academic base, the New School, Tim Marshall and Mary Watson's support has been invaluable.

Joseph Blasi at Rutgers University has been a generous friend and mentor. In addition, this book would not have been possible without the careful reading and comments of Morshed Mannan,

Jason Spicer, Fred Freundlich, Aman Bardia, Alissa Quart, Alexander Zaitchik, Lander Jimenez Ocio, and many others. Ultimately, my heartfelt gratitude goes to my partner, Jenny Perlin, and our children, Emma and Oliver, as well as our mostly adored feline pals, Ellie and Frankie, for their unfailing affection.

Notes

1. Alternative Paths

1. Mohammad Amir Anwar, Elly Otieno, and Malte Stein, "Locked In, Logged Out: Pandemic and Ride-Hailing in South Africa and Kenya," *Journal of Modern African Studies*, November 14, 2022, 1–22.

2. Raymond Williams, *Towards 2000—A Stimulating and Vigorous Assessment of the Choices That Face Our Society*, New Ed edition (Harmondsworth: Penguin, 1985), 105.

3. Noam Chomsky, "Platform Co-Ops Now with Noam Chomsky," Internet Archive, March 23, 2021, archive.org.

4. MSI Integrity, *Not Fit-for-Purpose: The Grand Experiment of Multi-Stakeholder Initiatives in Corporate Accountability, Human Rights and Global Governance* (Berkeley, CA: MSI Integrity, July 2020).

5. Chomsky, "Platform Co-Ops Now with Noam Chomsky"; Gaston Leval, *Collectives in the Spanish Revolution* (London: Freedom Press, 1975).

6. "Public Trust in Government: 1958–2022," Pew Research Center, June 6, 2021, pewresearch.org.

7. Yochai Benkler, *The Wealth of Networks* (Yale University Press, 2008), 275.

8. Jonathan Michie, Joseph R. Blasi, and Carlo Borzaga, "Introduction and Overview," in *The Oxford Handbook of Mutual, Co-Operative, and*

Co-Owned Business, ed. Jonathan Michie et al. (Oxford University Press, 2017).

9. "Household Internet Access: Number; 2019," Citizens' Committee for Children of New York (CCCNY) Database, data.cccnewyork.org.

10. "Platform Co-Op Directory," Platform Cooperativism Consortium, directory.platform.coop.

11. "Cooperative Identity, Values and Principles," International Cooperative Alliance Coop, ica.coop.

12. Mark Mather, Linda A. Jacobsen, and Kelvin M. Pollard, "Aging in the United States," *Population Bulletin* 70, no. 2 (2015).

13. PHI, *U.S. Home Care Workers: Key Facts* (New York: PHI, 2019).

14. "Labor Commissioner's Wage Theft Lawsuits against Uber and Lyft," State of California Department of Industrial Relations, updated October 2020, dir.ca.gov.

15. "Mission Statement," Park Slope Food Coop, foodcoop.com.

16. Alexandra Schwartz, "The Grocery Store Where Produce Meets Politics," *New Yorker*, November 25, 2019.

17. R. Trebor Scholz, "Platform Cooperativism vs. the Sharing Economy," *Medium*, December 5, 2014.

18. Marjorie Kelly, *Owning Our Future: The Emerging Ownership Revolution, Journeys to the Generative Economy* (San Francisco: Berrett-Koehler Publishers, 2012).

2. Worker Ownership for the Digital Economy

1. Julia Wolfe et al., *Domestic Workers Chartbook* (Washington, DC: Economic Policy Institute, 2014), 6–15.

2. Linda Burnham and Nick Theodore, *Home Economics: The Invisible and Unregulated World of Domestic Work* (New York: National Domestic Workers Alliance and Center for Urban Economic Development, 2012), 21.

3. Cirenia Dominguez, "Celebrating a Great Business Model for Immigrants on International Women's Day," *NYN Media*, March 8, 2018.

4. International Cooperative Alliance, "Aroundtheworld.Coop #8, Up & Go, New York, USA," ica.coop.

5. "Business Roundtable Redefines the Purpose of a Corporation to Promote 'An Economy That Serves All Americans,'" Business Roundtable, August 29, 2019.

6. Marc Benioff, "Marc Benioff: We Need a New Capitalism," *New York Times*, Opinion, October 14, 2019.

7. George Skelton, "It's No Wonder Hundreds of Millions Have Been Spent on Prop. 22. A Lot Is at Stake," *Los Angeles Times*, October 16, 2020.

8. Zephyr Teachout, *Break 'Em Up* (New York: St. Martin's Publishing Group, 2020).

9. "Who Owns Big Business: The Rise of Passive Investors (@uvaCORP-NET)," YouTube video, posted by Social Science Research/University of Amsterdam, November 3, 2016.

10. Jim Clifton, "The World's Broken Workplace," Gallup, June 13, 2017; Abha Bhattarai, "4.3 Million People Quit Their Jobs in January," *Washington Post*, March 9, 2022 (nearly 50 million Americans quit or changed jobs in 2021).

11. Dave Zirin, "Those Nonprofit Packers," *New Yorker*, January 25, 2011.

12. "What Is Employee Ownership?: Employment Stock Ownership Plans (ESOPs)," National Center for Employee Ownership (NCEO) webpage, nceo.org.

13. Reuters and SCMP Reporter, "Huawei Pays Out US$9.65 Billion in Dividends to Current and Retired Staff," *South China Morning Post*, April 5, 2022.

14. Trebor Scholz et al., "Policies for Cooperative Ownership in the Digital Economy," Platform Cooperativism Consortium, December 6, 2021.

15. Panu Kalmi, "The Disappearance of Cooperatives from Economics Textbooks," *Cambridge Journal of Economics* 31, no. 4 (July 2007): 625–47.

16. Trebor Scholz, Doug O'Brien, and Jason Spicer, "Can Cooperatives Build Worker Power?: Give Platform Co-ops a Seat at the Policy Table," *Public Seminar*, March 11, 2021.

17. Massimiliano Nicoli and Luca Paltrinieri, "Platform Cooperativism: Some Notes on the Becoming 'Common' of the Firm," *South Atlantic Quarterly* 118, no.4 (2019): 801–19.

18. Up & Go worker, interviewed by author.

19. Morshed Mannan, "Theorizing the Emergence of Platform Cooperativism: Drawing Lessons from Role-Set Theory," *Ondernemingsrecht* 2 (2022): 64–71.

20. Linda Burnham and Nick Theodore, *Home Economics: The Invisible and Unregulated World of Domestic Work*, National Domestic Workers Alliance and Center for Urban Economic Development, 2012, 21.

21. Wolfe et al., *Domestic Workers Chartbook*, 6–15.

22. Sylvia Morse, interviewed by the author, July 20, 2019.

23. Frank G. Runyeon, "Immigrants Fuel the Rise of Worker Cooperatives," *NYNMEDIA*, November 7, 2016.

24. Jessica Gordon Nembhard, *Collective Courage: A History of African American Cooperative Economic Thought and Practice* (Pennsylvania State University Press, 2014), 1.

25. Joseph R. Blasi, Douglas L. Kruse, and Richard B.Freeman, *The Citizen's Share: Reducing Inequality in the 21st Century* (New Haven, CT: Yale University Press, 2014), 191.

26. Shoshana Zuboff, *The Age of Surveillance Capitalism: The Fight for a Human Future at the New Frontier of Power* (New York: PublicAffairs, 2019).

27. "Sobre Mensakas" [About Mensakas], Mensakas, mensakas.com. See also "Qui Som" [Who are we?], Intersindical Alternativa de Catalunya (IAC), iac.cat.

3. Solidarity at Scale

1. Ernest Fritz Schumacher, *Small Is Beautiful: Economics as if People Mattered* (New York: Harper Perennial, 2014).

2. José van Dijck, Thomas Poell, and Martijn de Waal, *The Platform Society: Public Values in a Connective World* (New York: Oxford University Press, 2018), 30.

3. For more on this discussion, see Michele-Lee Moore, Darcy Riddell, and Dana Vocisano, "Scaling Out, Scaling Up, Scaling Deep: Strategies of Non-profits in Advancing Systemic Social Innovation," *Journal of Corporate Citizenship* 58 (June 2015): 67.

4. Jonathan Garlock, "Knights of Labor History and Geography 1869–1899," Mapping American Social Movements Project, University of Washington, depts.washington.edu/moves.

5. Trebor Scholz, "PCC & Mondragon University Offer Online Course to Incubate Platform Co-ops," Platform Cooperativism Consortium, May 20, 2020.

6. Jason S. Spicer, "Exceptionally Un-American? Why Co-Operative Enterprises Struggle in the United States, but Scale Elsewhere," (Phd. diss., Massachusetts Institute of Technology, 2018), 53.

7. J. David Goodman, "Amazon Pulls Out of Planned New York City Headquarters," *New York Times*, February 14, 2019, nytimes.com.

8. "AOC to Bezos, Billionaires: We Don't Want Your Money, But Your Power," YouTube video, posted by Tea Partiest, January 22, 2020. I co-authored an article with Casper Gelderblom discussing this: See Trebor Scholz and Casper Gelderblom, "Building an Alternative to Amazon? Toward a Planetary-Scale, Pluralist Commonwealth for the Digital Economy," *Public Seminar*, May 14, 2021.

9. Ibid.

10. Jack Kelly, "Senator Elizabeth Warren Says 'It's Time to Break Up Amazon, Google and Facebook'—and Facebook CEO Mark Zuckerberg Fights Back," *Forbes*, October 2, 2019; Mike Davis, "How to Save the Postal Service," *Nation*, April 6, 2020.

11. Neal Gorenflo, "How Platform Cooperatives Can Beat Death Stars Like Uber to Create a Real Sharing Economy," shareable.net, November 4, 2015.

12. Stacco Troncoso, in discussion with the author, July 22, 2020, and January 8, 2021.

13. Leo Sammallahti, "Maybe I'm biased because I'm in Finland where cooperatives have managed to outcompete their rivals . . .," Facebook, February 24, 2021.

14. See Deborah Gage, "The Venture Capital Secret: 3 out of 4 Start-Ups Fail," *Wall Street Journal*, September 20, 2012. See also Tom Eisenmann, "Why Start-Ups Fail," *Harvard Business Review*, September 17, 2021.

15. Federica Poli, *Co-operative Banking Networks in Europe: Models and Performance* (Cham: Palgrave Macmillan, 2019), chapters 1 and 9.

16. Gar Alperovitz, Thad Williamson, and Ted Howard, "The Cleveland Model," *Nation*, February 11, 2010.

17. Franco Mosconi and Andrea Montovi, "The 'Emilian Model' for the Twenty-First Century," paper prepared for the 12th European Network on Industrial Policy (EUNIP) International Conference, Faculty of Economics and Business, Universitat Rovira i Virgili, Reus, Spain, June 9–11, 2010.

18. Reiner Wandler, "Amazon auf Katalanisch" [Amazon in Catalan], *Die Tageszeitung*, February 3, 2021, taz.de.

19. Juliet Schor, *After the Gig: How the Sharing Economy Got Hijacked and How to Win It Back* (Oakland: University of California Press, 2020), 170.

20. "Jeremy Rifkin: Co-Op Models Could Lead the Digital Revolution," International Cooperative Alliance, October 27, 2016, ica.coop.

21. Cited in Zephyr Teachout and Bernard Sanders, *Break 'Em Up: Recovering Our Freedom from Big AG, Big Tech, and Big Money* (New York: All Points Books, 2020), 299.

22. Nick Srnicek, *Platform Capitalism* (Cambridge: Polity, 2019), 127.

23. Helen Scott, ed., *The Essential Rosa Luxemburg: Reform or Revolution and the Mass Strike* (Chicago: Haymarket Books, 2008).

24. Schor, *After the Gig*, 42.

25. "What Is a Co-Op? Definition of a Cooperative Business," NCBA CLUSA, February 2021.

26. Virginie Pérotin, *What Do We Really Know about Worker Co-operatives?* (Manchester, UK: Co-operatives UK, November 19, 2018), 5.

27. Hyung-sik Eum, *Cooperatives and Employment Second Global Report 2017* (Brussels: CICOPA, 2017), 85.

28. Dave Grace & Associates, *Measuring the Size and Scope of the Cooperative Economy: Results of the 2014 Global Census on Co-operatives* (United Nations' Division for Social Policy and Development, April 2014), 1.

29. Ibid., 2.

30. Michel Bauwens, "10 Ways to Accelerate the Peer-to-Peer and Commons Economy," shareable.net, March 4, 2019.

31. Liza Dessin, email message to the author, July 4, 2017.

32. "Smart en bref" [Smart in brief], Smart, smartbe.be.

33. Dessin, email, July 4, 2017.

34. Gar Alperovitz, *What Then Must We Do?: Straight Talk about the Next American Revolution* (Hartford, VT: Chelsea Green Publishing, 2013), 14.

35. "Historique" [History], Smart, smartbe.be.

36. Dessin, email, July 4, 2017.

37. Idee in Movimento, "Associazione Rappresentanza Studentesca: 'Idee in Movimento' Università degli Studi di Perugia," Facebook page.

38. "Servizio di consegne a domicilio a Bologna," Consegne Etiche, consegnetiche.it.

39. Marco Lombardo, "La carta dei diritti fondamentali del lavoro digitale nel contesto urbano" [Charter of fundamental rights of digital workers], Forum Disuguaglianze Diversità [Forum on inequality and diversity], November 11, 2019, forumdisuguaglianzediversita.org.

40. Peter S. Goodman, "Co-ops in Spain's Basque Region Soften Capitalism's Rough Edges," *New York Times*, December 29, 2020; David Herrera, "Mondragon: A For-profit Organization that Embodies Catholic Social Thought," *Review of Business* 25, no. 1 (2004): 56.

41. Lawrence Mishel and Jori Kandra, *CEO Compensation Surged 14% in 2019 to $21.3 Million: CEOs Now Earn 320 Times as Much as a Typical Worker* (Washington, DC: Economic Policy Institute, 2018).

42. Marcelo Vieta, *Workers' Self-Management in Argentina: Contesting Neo-Liberalism by Occupying Companies Creating Cooperatives, and Recuperating Autogestión* (Leiden: Brill, 2019), 517–19.

43. Jennifer Brandel, Mara Zepeda, Astrid Scholz, and Aniyia Wiliam, "Zebras Fix What Unicorns Break," *Medium*, July 13, 2017.

44. Cited in Jason S. Spicer, "Exceptionally Un-American? Why Co-operative Enterprises Struggle in the United States, but Scale Elsewhere," (Phd diss., Massachusetts Institute of Technology, 2018), 102. See also Alex

Gourevitch, *From Slavery to the Cooperative Commonwealth: Labor and Republican Liberty in the Nineteenth Century* (Cambridge: Cambridge University Press, 2015).

45. "SEWA Cooperative Federation in India: Towards Self-Reliance," International Labour Organization, August 16, 2017, ilo.org.

46. Salonie Muralidhara Hiriyur, "Designing Agricultural Platform Cooperatives with Women Farmers in Gujarat," Institute for the Cooperative Digital Economy, Research Reports, March 14, 2022.

47. Karen Fulbright-Anderson, Patricia Auspos, and Andrea Anderson, "Community Involvement in Partnerships with Educational Institutions, Medical Centers, and Utility Companies," paper presented at the Aspen Institute Roundtable on Comprehensive Community Initiatives for the Annie E. Casey Foundation, January 2001.

48. See the example of BlaBlacar, which is now in part owned by the French government. Chris O'Brien, "Blablacar Buys French Bus Service, Raises $114 Million," *VentureBeat*, November 12, 2018.

49. Thomas T. M. Isaac and Michelle Williams, *Building Alternatives: The Story of India's Oldest Construction Workers' Cooperative* (New Delhi: LeftWord, 2017), 40.

4. Redefining Value

1. Tyler Cowen, *Average Is Over: Powering America Beyond the Age of the Great Stagnation* (New York: Penguin Group, 2014), 23.

2. Ibid.

3. McKinsey & Company, *McKinsey on COOPERATIVES* (McKinsey & Company Industry Publications, Autumn 2012), 2.

4. "The Cooperative Movement in Kenya," Co-operative Housing International, housinginternational.coop.

5. John Restakis, *Humanizing the Economy: Co-operatives in the Age of Capital* (Gabriola Island, BC: New Society Publishers, 2010), 55–8; John Duda, "The Italian Region Where Co-ops Produce a Third of Its GDP," *Yes!*, July 5, 2016.

6. Simon Rogers, "Bobby Kennedy on GDP: 'Measures Everything Except That Which Is Worthwhile,'" *Guardian*, May 24, 2012.

7. Sanjay Reddy, "Facts and Values Are Entangled: Deal With It," interview by Perry G. Mehrling, Institute for New Economic Thinking, January 9, 2012, stage2.ineteconomics.org.

8. Christian Kroll and Sebastian Pokutta, "Just a Perfect Day? Developing a Happiness Optimized Day Schedule," *Journal of Economic Psychology* 34 (2013): 215.

9. Reddy, "Facts and Values Are Entangled."

10. Ibid.

11. Bryce Covert, "Putting a Price Tag on Unpaid Housework," *Forbes*, May 30, 2012. The article points out that if only domestic work were to be included in the GDP, it would have increased it by 26 percent in 2010.

12. Tithi Bhattacharya, "What Is Social Reproduction Theory?," socialist-worker.org, September 10, 2013; "Diane Coyle on the Shortcomings of GDP," December 8, 2017, in *IMF PODCASTS*, by International Monetary Fund, MP3 audio; Bob Simison, "People in Economics: Economics Agitator (Mariana Mazzucato)," *Finance and Development* 57 (2020): 48–51.

13. "How to Restore Trust in Government" | Jason Saul | TEDx Chicago," YouTube video, posted by TEDx Talks, August 20, 2018.

14. Ewan Robertson, "Venezuela's Maduro Creates Social Happiness Ministry, Is Criticised by International Media," *Venezuelanalysis.com*, October 28, 2013; "Buen Vivir: The Rights of Nature in Bolivia and Ecuador," Rapid Transition Alliance, December 2, 2018, rapidtransition.org.

15. Graham Mitchell, "meet.coop is solid and stable—I use it regularly for two hour long calls and it just works," Facebook, May 4, 2021.

16. IKEA reference from Melissa Hoover's presentation in "Digital Co-op Fractals: Iterations, Patterns, Questions," Who Owns the World? The State of Platform Cooperativism, Platform Cooperativism Consortium conference, New York, November 7–9, 2019.

17. Jessica Gordon Nembhard, *Collective Courage: A History of African American Cooperative Economic Thought and Practice* (University Park: Pennsylvania State University Press, 2014), 14.

18. Robynn Cox, "Applying the Theory of Social Good to Mass Incarceration and Civil Rights," *Research on Social Work Practice* 30, no. 2 (2020): 205–18.

19. Daniel Cahill, in discussion with the author, December 17, 2020.

20. Alison Griswold, "Dirty Work: Almost Everything that Start-Ups Get Right—and Horribly Wrong—Happened at Home-Cleaning Service Handy," *Slate*, July 24, 2015; "Occupational Employment and Wages, May 2019: 37-2012 Maids and Housekeeping Cleaners," Bureau of Labor Statistics, bls.gov.

21. "New Home Services Platform Up & Go Shakes Up the Gig Economy by Putting Workers in Charge," Robinhood, May 10, 2017, robinhood.org; Marjorie Kelly, *Owning Our Future: The Emerging Ownership Revolution, Journeys to the Generative Economy* (Oakland: Berrett-Koehler Publishers, 2012), 16.

22. Juliet Schor, *After the Gig: How the Sharing Economy Got Hijacked and How to Win It Back* (Oakland: University of California Press, 2020), 166.

23. "Open Budget," Barcelona Digital City, ajuntament.barcelona.cat/digital.

24. Ernst Hafen, "Personal Data Cooperatives—A New Data Governance Framework for Data Donations and Precision Health," in *The Ethics of Medical Data Donation*, ed. Jenny Krutzinna and Luciano Floridi (Cham: Springer, 2019).

25. Gallup, *State of the Global Workplace* (New York: Gallup Press, 2017), 25–40

26. Virginie Pérotin, *What Do We Really Know about Worker Co-operatives?* (Manchester: Co-operatives UK, 2021), 18–20; Ed Mayo, "The International Co-operative Alliance and Platform Co-ops: Options for the ICA to Support Platform Co-ops in Its Forward Strategy," discussion paper, International Co-operative Alliance, February 1, 2019, 15–19.

27. Gabriel Burdín, "Are Worker-Managed Firms More Likely to Fail Than Conventional Enterprises? Evidence from Uruguay," *ILR Review* 67, no. 1 (January 2014): 209–27; Erik K. Olsen, "The Relative Survival of Worker Cooperatives and Barriers to Their Creation," in *Sharing Ownership,*

Profits, and Decision-Making in the 21st Century, ed. Douglas Kruse (UK: Emerald Group Publishing Limited, 2013).

28. Bryn Glover, "What Is a Startup Cooperative Business?," startups.co.uk, May 12, 2021.

29. Joseph Cureton, in discussion with the author, January 7, 2021.

30. Sasha Costanza-Chock, *Design Justice: Community-Led Practices to Build the Worlds We Need* (Cambridge, MA: MIT Press, 2020), 111.

31. Chenai Chair, "Feminist Imaginings for Fair Platforms," fairbnb.coop, May 20, 2021.

32. Safiya Umoja Noble, *Algorithms of Oppression: How Search Engines Reinforce Racism* (New York: New York University Press, 2018), 2.

33. Trebor Scholz, "Brazilian Recycling Workers, or Catadores, Envision a Fairer Future through a New Platform Co-op," Platform Cooperativism Consortium blog, September 3, 2018, platform.coop.

34. Heira Hardiyanti, in discussion with the author, June 9, 2022.

35. "The Transformation of the Cooperative Movement Massively Strengthens the Main Pillar of the Nation's Economy," news release, Coordinating Ministry for Economic Affairs, Republic of Indonesia, July 1, 2022, ekon. go.id.

36. "Young People and Cooperatives: A New Report Seeks to Improve Engagement between Young People and the Cooperative Movement," International Co-operative Alliance, March 3, 2021, ica.coop.

37. Trebor Scholz, "Platform Co-op Movement Gathers in Hong Kong for Its Global Conference," *Co-op News*, November 8, 2016, thenews.coop.

38. Cahill, in discussion, December 17, 2020.

39. Marjorie Kelly, *Owning Our Future: The Emerging Ownership Revolution, Journeys to the Generative Economy* (Oakland: Berrett-Koehler Publishers, 2012), 9.

40. Co-operatives UK, *The Co-operative Economy 2018* (Manchester: Co-operatives UK, 2018).

41. Vera Negri Zamagni, in discussion with the author, December 1, 2020.

42. Michele Bianchi and Marcelo Vieta, "Italian Community Co-operatives Responding to Economic Crisis and State Withdrawal: A New Model for

Socio-Economic Development"" (paper presented at the UNTFSSE International Conference, Geneva, June 25–6, 2019).

43. Alexander Billet, "Spotify's Streaming Model Is Based on Exploitation," *Jacobin*, December 8, 2020.

44. Jari Muikku, "Pro Rata and User Centric Distribution Models: A Comparative Study," *Digital Media Finland*, November 30, 2017, 9.

45. "About," Catalytic Sound, catalyticsound.com; Andy Cush, "Meet the Experimental Musicians Who Built Their Own Streaming Service," *Pitchfork*, March 25, 2021, pitchfork.com; "Welcome!: Documentation Overview," Ampled, docs.ampled.com.

46. Ibid.

47. Ibid.

48. "It's a Co-op," Resonate, resonate.coop/coop.

49. Rich Jensen, in discussion with the author, December 14, 2020.

50. International Cooperative Alliance, "Brazil," coops4dev.coop.

51. Edward S. Herman and Noam Chomsky, *Manufacturing Consent: The Political Economy of the Mass Media* (New York: Pantheon Books, 1988), 306.

52. Nathan Schneider, "Broad-Based Stakeholder Ownership in Journalism: Co-ops, ESOPs, Blockchains," *Media Industries* 7, no. 2 (2020).

53. "CIVIL—Decentralized Marketplace for Sustainable Journalism with Cofounder Matt Coolidge," YouTube video, posted by Inchained, June 12, 2018.

54. Kate Clark, "Blockchain Media Startup Civil Is Issuing Full Refunds to All Buyers of Its Cryptocurrency," *TechCrunch*, October 16, 2018.

55. "Ending the Civil Journey," Civil, civil.co.

56. Pérotin, *What Do We Really Know about Worker Co-operatives?*; Mayo, "The International Co-operative Alliance and Platform Co-ops."

5. Roots of Resilience: Unions and Platform Cooperatives

1. Riders x Derechos website, ridersxderechos.org.

2. David O'Connell, in discussion with the author, July 28, 2021.

3. Carmen Molinari, "You Can't Win without a Fight: Why Worker Cooperatives Are a Bad Strategy," *Organizing Work*, January 29, 2021.

4. Ibid.

5. Ellerman, David P. "The Legitimate Opposition at Work: The Union's Role in Large Democratic Firms," *Economic and Industrial Democracy* 9, no. 4 (November 1, 1988): 437–53.

6. Elizabeth A. Hoffmann. "Confrontations and Compromise: Dispute Resolution at a Worker Cooperative Coal Mine," *Law and Social Inquiry* 26, no. 3 (Summer 2001): 568.

7. Michele Bianchi and Marcelo Vieta, "Italian Community Co-Operatives Responding to Economic Crisis and State Withdrawal: A New Model for Socio-Economic Development," *SSRN Electronic Journal*, January 2019; Istituto Nazionale di Statistica, "Poverty in Italy: Year 2021," July 7, 2022, istat.it.

8. Jamie Woodcock and Mark Graham, *The Gig Economy: A Critical Introduction* (Cambridge: Polity, 2020), 23.

9. Ra Criscitiello, "There Is Platform-Power in a Union," *Ours to Hack and to Own: The Rise of Platform Cooperativism, A New Vision for the Future of Work and a Fairer Internet*, ed. Trebor Scholz and Nathan Schneider (New York: OR Books, 2017).

10. Woodcock and Graham, *The Gig Economy*, 76.

11. SEIU-UHW, "SEIU-UHW: Leading for Healthcare in California and Beyond," seiu-uhw.org/about-seiu-uhw.

12. International Alliance of App-Based Transport Workers website, iaatw.org.

13. Woodcock and Graham, *The Gig Economy*, 184; Bradford Gray, Dana O. Sarnak, and Jako Burgers, *Home Care by Self-Governing Nursing Teams: The Netherlands' Buurtzorg Model* (New York: The Commonwealth Fund, May 29, 2015).

14. World Health Organization, "Ageing and Health," fact sheet, October 1, 2022, who.int.

15. American Hospital Association, "Fact Sheet: Strengthening the Health Care Workforce," November 2021, aha.org.

16. Ashley Kirzinger et al., *KFF/The Washington Post Frontline Health Care Workers Survey* (*Washington Post*/KFF Survey Project, April 6, 2021), 14–16.

17. SEIU-UHW, "Leading for Healthcare in California and Beyond."

18. Nithin Coca, "Nurses Join Forces with Labor Union to Launch Healthcare Platform Cooperative," shareable.net, August 21, 2017.

19. Helen Duplessis, email message to the author.

20. Coca, "Nurses Join Forces with Labor Union."

21. Ibid.

22. According to the US Bureau of Labor Statistics, the mean wage for licensed vocational nurses in the US in May 2020 was US$30.81. Bureau of Labor Statistics, "Occupational Employment and Wage Statistics, May 2020: 29-2061 Licensed Practical and Licensed Vocational Nurses," bls.gov.

23. Gerald L. Maatman Jr. et al., "Online Health Care Job Platforms— Worker Misclassification Risks," American Staffing Agency, June 2022, americanstaffing.net.

24. Minsun Ji, "Platform Worker Organizing," Institute for the Cooperative Digital Economy, Research Reports, December 21, 2020, 17.

25. Independent Drivers Guild, "Benefits," driversguild.org/benefits.

26. Erik Forman, *Top Dead Center: The Drivers Cooperative, Capitalism, and the Next Revolution* (New York: Platform Cooperativism Consortium, 2022), 32.

27. Daryl Leeworthy, *Labour Country: Political Radicalism and Social Democracy in South Wales 1831–1985* (Cardigan, UK: Parthian Books, 2020).

28. John Curl, *For All the People: Uncovering the Hidden History of Cooperation, Cooperative Movements, and Communalism in America* (Oakland: PM Press, 2012), 111.

29. Victor Drury, *The Polity of the Labor Movement* (Philadelphia: Frederick Turner, 1885), 149.

30. Nathan Schneider, *Everything for Everyone: The Radical Tradition That Is Shaping the Next Economy* (New York: PublicAffairs, 2018), 86.

31. Jessica Gordon Nembhard, *Collective Courage: A History of African American Cooperative Economic Thought and Practice* (University Park: Pennsylvania State University Press, 2014), 51.

32. Rebecca Lurie and Bernadette King Fitzsimons, *A Union Toolkit for Cooperative Solutions* (Community and Worker Ownership Project at the CUNY School of Labor and Union Studies, 2021).

33. James Felton Keith, "Data Is Labor: Why We Need Data Unions," Coin-Desk, November 15, 2020, coindesk.com.

34. Eric A. Posner and E. Glen Weyl, *Radical Markets: Uprooting Capitalism and Democracy for a Just Society* (Princeton, NJ: Princeton University Press, 2019), 205–49.

35. Salonie Muralidhara Hiriyur, *Designing Agriculture Platform Cooperatives with Women Farmers in Gujarat* (New York: Platform Cooperativism Consortium, 2022), 7.

36. Mirai Chatterjee, in discussion with the author, July 7, 2021.

37. Ibid.

38. Platform Cooperative Consortium, "The People's Disruption: Platform Co-ops for Global Challenges," conference webpage, 2017, platform.coop.

39. Victoria Basualdo et al., *Building Workers' Power in Digital Capitalism: Old and New Labour Struggles* (Bonn: Friedrich-Ebert-Stiftung, 2021).

40. GMB Union, "New Co-operative Puts Power Back in the Hands of Drivers," March 1, 2019, gmb.org.uk.

6. The Coming Data Democracy

1. "Cooperativas pesqueras: Un modelo que aporta a la seguridad alimentaria," Secretariat of Agriculture and Rural Development blog, July 6, 2020, gob.mx/agricultura.

2. Stuart Fulton and Ines Lopez (COBI), in discussion with the author, October 24, 2022.

3. COBI, *Annual Report 2021* (Guaymas, Sonora: Comunidad y Biodiversidad A.C., 2022), cobi.org.mx.

4. Fulton and Lopez, in discussion, October 24, 2022.

5. Ines Lopez, email message to the author, October 24, 2022.

6. Ines Lopez, in discussion with the author, October 24, 2022.

7. Ibid.

8. "About: A Grower's Data Coop—Leveling the Growing Field," GiSC website, accessed November 26, 2021, web.archive.org/web/20220528005644/https://www.gisc.coop/about.

9. Jason Wiener || p.c., "Closing Out Cooperative Month with Kat Kuzmeskas of Shyro," medium.com, November 9, 2022.

10. "Our Mission," CoMetrics, cometrics.com/our-mission.

11. Bianca Wylie and Sean McDonald, "What Is a Data Trust?," Centre for International Governance Innovation, October 9, 2018, cigionline.org.

12. Sylvie Delacroix and Neil D. Lawrence, "Bottom-Up Data Trusts: Disturbing the 'One Size Fits All' Approach to Data Governance," *International Data Privacy Law* 9, no. 4 (2019): 242.

13. Nithin Coca, "Moeda: The Cooperative Cryptocurrency That Aims to Advance Financial Inclusion," shareable.net, December 20, 2017.

14. Giustino Di Cecco, "V: Venture Capital for Co-operatives," in *The Cooperative Firm: Keywords*, ed. Andrea Bernardi and Salvatore Monni (Rome: RomaTr*E*-*Press*, 2016), 153–8.

15. Christian Buggedei and Felix Dahlke, "In Pod We Trust: Toward a Transparent Data Economy" (white paper, polypoly.coop, November 25, 2020), 9.

16. Ibid., 36.

17. For a discussion of this prospect see Morshed Mannan, Janis Wong, and Elettra Bietti, "Data Cooperatives in Europe: A Preliminary Investigation," *Network Industries Quarterly* 24, no. 3 (July 2022): 12–15.

18. Mario Tronti, "Factory and Society," *Operaismo in English* (blog), June 13, 2013, operaismoinenglish.wordpress.com.

19. Trebor Scholz, *Uberworked and Underpaid: How Workers Are Disrupting the Digital Economy* (Cambridge: Polity, 2017), 104.

20. Alex Pentland and Thomas Hardjono, "2. Data Cooperatives," in *Building the New Economy*, ed. Alex Pentland, Alexander Lipton, and Thomas Hardjono, MIT Press Works in Progress, April 30, 2020, wip.mitpress.mit.edu.

21. Yakov Feygin et al., *A Data Dividend That Works: Steps Toward Building an Equitable Data Economy* (Los Angeles, Berggruen Institute, May 5, 2021), 5.

22. Ibid., 11.

23. Paul Wolman, "The New Deal for Energy in the United States 1930–
    1950," in *The Challenge of Rural Electrification: Strategies for Developing
    Countries,* ed. Douglas Barnes (Washington, DC: Resources for the
    Future, 2007), 259–92.

24. "We Are America's Electric Cooperatives," NRECA, electric.coop/
    our-mission/americas-electric-cooperatives.

25. "The Digital Services Act Package," European Commission, digital-
    strategy.ec.europa.eu.

26. Te Mana Raraunga, "Principles of Māori Data Sovereignty," Brief #1
    (October 2018), temanararaunga.maori.nz.

27. James Charlton, *Nothing About Us Without Us: Disability Oppression and
    Empowerment* (Berkeley: University of California Press, 2000).

28. Eden Medina, *Cybernetic Revolutionaries: Technology and Politics in Allende's
    Chile,* reprint edition (Cambridge, MA: MIT Press, 2014).

29. Luis Bergolla, Karen Seif, and Can Eken, "Kleros: A Socio-Legal Case
    Study of Decentralized Justice and Blockchain Arbitration," *Ohio State
    Journal on Dispute Resolution* 55 (2022).

30. Anna Grignani et al., "Community Cooperative: A New Legal Form for
    Enhancing Social Capital for the Development of Renewable Energy
    Communities in Italy," *Energies* 14, no. 21 (January 2021): 7029.

31. Alanna Irving, "Social.coop: A Cooperative Decentralized Social Net-
    work," medium.com, August 28, 2017.

32. Cameron Burgess et al., *A Rising Tide Lifts All Boats: How Mobilising
    Knowledge between Marine Conservation Organisations Can Support Large-
    Scale Marine Conservation Outcomes in Latin America and the Caribbean*
    (Guaymas, Sonora: Comunidad y Biodiversidad A.C., 2022), cobi.org.mx.

33. Quoted in Irving, "Social.Coop."

34. Eli Zeger, "Working at the Faux-Op," *Baffler,* July 1, 2021, thebaffler.com.

35. Holochain, "Why Holochain?," holochain.org/why-holochain.

36. Holochain, "Projects," holochain.org/projects.

37. Alex Pentland, Alexander Lipton, and Thomas Hardjono, *Building the
    New Economy: Data as Capital* (Cambridge, MA: MIT Press, 2021), 20.

38. Ibid., 23.

39. Isabelle Allemand, Bénédicte Brullebaut, Anne-Sophie Louis, and Emmanuel Zenou, "The Construction of Democracy in Cooperative Banks," *RIMHE: Revue Interdisciplinaire Management, Homme & Entreprise* 45, 10, no. 4 (2021): 3a–25a.

40. Nabil Hassein, "Against Black Inclusion in Facial Recognition," *Digital Talking Drum* (blog), August 15, 2017, digitaltalkingdrum.com.

41. Nathan Schneider, "Web3 Is the Opportunity We Have Had All Along: Innovation Amnesia and Economic Democracy" (unpublished manuscript, July 13, 2022), available at nathanschneider.info/open-work; Emmi Bevensee, Jahed Momand, and Frank Miroslav, "No Ethical Activism under Capitalism: DAOs, DeFi, and Purity Politics," Center for a Stateless Society, December 17, 2021, c4ss.org.

42. Patrick McGinty, "There Is No Leftist Case for Crypto," *Jacobin*, October 22, 2022.

43. Ryan Browne, "Web Inventor Tim Berners-Lee Wants Us to 'Ignore' Web3: 'Web3 Is Not the Web At All,'" cnbc.com, November 4, 2022.

44. Solid website, solid.mit.edu.

45. Dmytri Kleiner, "Counterantidisintermediation," in *Ours to Hack and to Own: The Rise of Platform Cooperativism, A New Vision for the Future of Work and a Fairer Internet*, ed. Trebor Scholz and Nathan Schneider (New York: OR Books, 2017).

7. Letter from 2035

1. André Gorz, *Strategy for Labor: A Radical Proposal* (Boston: Beacon Press, 1967), 4–5.

Epilogue

1. Greg Brodsky, email message to the author, November 16, 2022.

2. Simy Joy and Priya Nair Rajeev, *Platform Co-op Markets? Insights from Kudumbashree in Kerala* (New York: Platform Cooperativism Consortium and the New School India China Institute, 2022).

3. "How to Start a Platform Co-op," Co-operatives UK, uk.coop.

4. Greg Brodsky, email message to the author, November 4, 2022.

5. Vasilis Kostakis and Michel Bauwens, "Cooperativism in the Digital Era, or How to Form a Global Counter-economy," openDemocracy, March 6, 2017, opendemocracy.net.

6. Drivers Cooperative, "Our Mission," drivers.coop/about-us.

7. Kristin Toussaint, "How the Drivers Cooperative built a worker-owned alternative to Uber and Lyft," *Fast Company*, July 15, 2021, fastcompany.com.

8. "Access-a-Ride: Ways to Do the Right Thing More Efficiently," Citizens Budget Commission, September 20, 2016, cbcny.org.

Index